Karma

and

Creativity

Karma

and

Creativity

Christopher Chapple

State University of New York Press

Published by
State University of New York Press, Albany

Printed in the United States of America

For information, address State University of New York Press, State University Plaza, Albany, N.Y., 12246

Library of Congress Cataloging-in-Publication Data

Chapple, Christopher.
Karma and creativity.

Bibliography: p.
Includes index.
1. Karma. 2. Hinduism—Doctrines. I. Title.
BL2015.K3C46 1986 294.5'22 85-17339
ISBN 0-88706-250-4
ISBN 0-88706-251-2 (pbk.)

10 9 8 7 6 5

to Gurāṇi Añjali

SUNY Series in Religion

Robert C. Neville, Editor

Contents

Acknowledgements

I am grateful to several people who have assisted in the birthing of this small volume. The members of my dissertation committee at Fordham University — John B. Chethimattam, Anne Feldhaus, and Thomas Berry — helped see me through that critical first passage into the fields of theology and indology. C.T. Shen, Richard A. Gard, Christopher S. George, Hannah Robinson, Janet Gyatso, Lorraine Frey, and Jane Abritis, my former colleagues at the Institute for Advanced Studies of World Religions, have been immensely supportive. Concurrently, many insights and much encouragement were received from colleagues and friends at the State University of New York at Stony Brook, including Antonio T. deNicolás, Thomas J.J. Altizer, Steve Odin, Sal Familia, Robert Goldenberg, Robert C. Neville, Sung-bae Park, and Peter Manchester. I am especially grateful to my wife, Maureen Shannon Chapple, and to the staff of Yoga Anand Ashram, particularly Yogi Anand Virāj and Gurāṇi Añjali. It was one brief epigram spoken by Gurāṇi Añjali that served as the seed which prompted the fruit that follows: "Desire is the root of creation. As you will, so you will be."

Christopher Chapple
Department of Theology
Loyola Marymount University
Los Angeles, California

Preface

The word *karma* has become part of the English language. From the lyrics of popular music to sometimes fantastic accountings for otherwise unexplainable occurrences, the concept of karma has found a home in contemporary Western culture. In the process, it has come to be understood as equivalent to fate and associated with forces beyond human control. It is also used freely and interchangeably with notions of reincarnation. However, this array of meanings and implications adds a great deal to the Sanskrit definition and textual usage of the word; in its pure sense, karma simply refers to action. Because texts mentioning karma often state that actions of the past and present will carry over and influence actions of the future, some interpretors have seen only damning possibilities in this operation. However, the mechanics of karma can also be regarded as incentive to better oneself, to strive to create action in a purposeful fashion. To rekindle memory of the latter interpretation of karma, this book provides a tour through several texts of Indian religious traditions that discuss human action in a positive light. These include portions of Vedic and Upaniṣadic literature, the *Mahābhārata*, the *Yoga Sūtra*, the *Sāṃkhya Kārikā*, and, most importantly, the *Yogavāsiṣṭha*. It is hoped that the approach taken will help clarify the importance of action in the history of Indian thought, providing documentation of karma as a life affirming principle as opposed to its often pessimistic presentation in modern parlance.

1

The Problem of Action

The religious traditions of India seem to consistently dip into the paradoxical. On the one hand, it is asserted that all action leads to suffering, the world is impure and impermanent; true knowledge can only be found outside the confines of conventionality, away from the realm of action. On the other hand, the same texts and traditions extol human activity as the only vehicle for highest knowledge. According to some schools of thought, liberation, self-realization, inherent Buddha-nature, and *nirvāṇa* are achievable in this lifetime by performing particular types of action. The question may be asked, what is the relationship between these two positions? Can abnegation of action be reconciled with the advocacy of action for a higher purpose?

Within the classical texts of what may be broadly termed the Indian tradition, religious understanding exhibits a dialectical reciprocity. Seemingly antagonistic perspectives on human life actually complement one another: *saṃsāra/nirvāṇa, duḥkha/sukha,* inaction/action. Suffering *(duḥkha)* binds one to further ignorance and aimless wandering *(saṃsāra)* in the domain of compulsive action. However, this same suffering can prompt one to desire transcendence, to strive for liberation or enlightenment *(nirvāṇa)*, allowing one to act freely, as if doing nothing at all. But before this state can be attained, the root cause of actions that lead to suffering must be sought out and, through purificatory actions, set aside. This is the crux of the Indian philosophical endeavor: to see the dissatisfaction inherent in the changes of life and then to find a process by which this dissatisfaction may be apprehended. Various paths to achieve this goal have been prescribed by numerous teachers, from the Jaina adherence to nonviolence *(ahiṃsā)* to the Vaisnavite's devotion to Sri Krishna. Regardless of method, each school focuses on the transformation of human action from modes rooted in ignorance *(avidyā)* resulting in suffering, to a way of life which minimizes self-concern *(asmitā)* and compulsive attraction and revulsion *(rāga/dveṣa)*. The cornerstone of religious practice is the doctrine of karma: that our actions in the past converge in the present and shape our future life.

The word karma has become a household term worldwide and is defined in the *Oxford English Dictionary* as "The sum of a person's actions in one of his successive states of existence, regarded as determining his fate in the next; hence, necessary fate or destiny following as effect from cause." This definition refers to a popularized Western interpretation of the word developed by Theosophists and turn of the century Orientalists. Actually, this definition of karma as fate or destiny denotes something additional to the meaning of the word *karma* in Sanskrit. Derived from the verbal root *kṛ* (do, make, perform, accomplish), karma is the nominative singular form of the neuter word *karman*, which means "act, action, performance, deed." In grammatical usage, *karman* refers to the direct object in a sentence, the recipient of the action indicated by the verb. Hence, strictly speaking, karma is no more than action itself. When the term is used, any judgment as to the nature of the action performed or statements about its origins or implications would require additional explanation. Karma, in and of itself, carries no negative connotations and does not imply any particular cosmological view. Although certain schools have developed diverse theories about action, the interpretation of karma offered in English lexicons and indicated by its common usage in popular culture is misleading. The fallout of the usage of the term karma in colloquial English has been a universal association of Indian philosophy with a resignation that one's lot in life is irreversible and inherently miserable.

Furthermore, the concept of karma has become linked with the idea of reincarnation, despite the fact that the Sanskrit term for reincarnation *(punar janma)* is etymologically unrelated to the word karma or its verbal root *kṛ*. Some scholars have gone to great lengths to disassociate karma from reincarnation, emphasizing that the latter does not appear in Vedic literature and that even in contemporary Indian society, Hindus regard karma primarily as ritual action and do not immediately link the notion of karma with notions of rebirth.[1]

Nonetheless, the idea that one life transforms into another after death is an integral part of the post-Vedic Hindu tradition and is found in both Jainism and Buddhism. In Buddhism, memory of past lives is said to arise spontaneously when certain meditational states are achieved or when prescribed devotional rituals are performed.[2] In the Hindu tradition, perhaps the earliest hint of the notion of rebirth is found in the *Bṛhadāraṇyaka Upaniṣad*, contemporaneous with the rise of Buddhism:

> Now as a caterpillar, when it has come to the end of a blade of grass, in taking the next step draws itself together towards it, just so this soul in taking the next step strikes down this body, dispels its ignorance, and draws itself together.[3]

Śankara, in his commentary on the *Brahmasūtra*, interprets this passage as indicating how the actions from one lifetime are carried into the next.

The doctrine of reincarnation did not gain widespread acceptance in Hinduism until the time of the *Dharmaśāstras*. Compiled from about 200 B.C.E. onwards, these texts outlined various means to regulate society based on Brahmanical teachings. Detailed catalogues were given of which acts *(karman)* produce corresponding fruits *(phala)* in the form of future births *(janma)*. For instance, according to the *Laws of Manu*, if one kills a brahman, then one is reborn as a dog, a pig, a camel, a cow, a goat, a sheep, a deer, a bird, an untouchable, or a mixed-birth tribal. Thieves are reborn as spiders, snakes, lizards, or aquatic animals. Various actions are prescribed in the *Laws of Manu* and other texts for overcoming the influence of impure acts to avoid such destinies.[4] Similarly, the Buddhist *Avadāna Śataka* tells of a group of lazy and indolent students who were reborn as parrots and swans for failing to keep up their duties.[5] The lesson, obviously, is that students should study more assiduously.

The mass psychology of such "karmic" tales undoubtedly served to regulate social behavior and helped establish and maintain the highly stratified caste system and its attendant laws and system of punishments. Futhermore, for the great majority of Hindus, life certainly was not pleasant and this lore helped bring a degree of acceptance of human suffering. However, this method of coping was regarded by the outside world as nothing less than repugnant. At the turn of the century, the approach to karma that tends to explain all phenomena in terms of retribution for past actions provoked Farquhar to write that "the theory of karma. . . checks seriously the natural flow of human kindliness and puts grave obstacles in the way of the use of philanthropy. Beneficence could only act in spite of the law of karma."[6] The theory of karma was seen as a tool used to reinforce societal injustice and discourage efforts to better oneself or to help others.

However, the stagnation often associated with so-called karmic interpretations of life is only half the picture. It is indeed true that the doctrine of karma played an important role in the establishment and concretizing of the caste system. But a parallel system also developed which asserts that through human effort all the shackles of karma can be cast aside. Contrary to the opinion of those who hold the notion of karma responsible for so-called Indian pessimism, the doctrine of bondage due to past actions was for many a call for action in the present, a necessary precursor to the possibility of liberation. These individuals developed highly sophisticated techniques for overcoming the influences of past action through the application of ethical, psychological, and meditative practices.

The seminal text on liberative technique in Indian philosophy is the *Yoga Sūtra,* which will be discussed in more detail in a later chapter. A cluster of aphorisms from this text, paraphrased as follows, outlines the basic thrust of the mechanics of karma and its fruits. The central premise is that karma is associated with affliction *(kleśa).* Rooted in ignorance *(avidyā),* afflicted action causes the repeated arising of situations or births, durations of experience, and enjoyments. Depending upon whether acts are virtuous or nonvirtuous, karma produces pleasant or unpleasant results.[7] Every action *(karman)* leaves a residue *(saṃskāra,* also from the verbal root *kṛ)* in the memory of a person. These residues or traces collectively form habit patterns *(vāsanā,* from the root *vas,* dwell) that dictate personality: how one perceives and reacts to the world. For the average person, rooted in impressions formed in the past that are linked to various afflictions *(kleśa),* life is an unending accumulation and fruition of actions caused by craving and ignorance. The yogin, on the other hand, strives to become impervious to all forms of action. Through the practices of yoga, the influence of action as dictated by the afflictions of human weakness are lessened to the point where, though seemingly involved with all activity, the yogin or yoginī is internally peaceful and not bound by what otherwise appears to be worldly existence. Due to his or her meditative accomplishments, karma is said to be neither white (virtuous) nor black (nonvirtuous) nor mixed.[8] Nonattachment, as we will see in texts from various traditions, is the key to the transcendence of afflicted action.

Despite the universal quality of yogic teachings, during the earliest phases of Hinduism this state of liberation was only accessible to the Brahmans who had renounced society and taken up the life of the forest dweller. Having seen the birth of their children's children, and having accomplished the goals of wealth *(artha),* sensual fulfillment *(kāma),* and societal duty *(dharma),* they would hand over their duties to the next generation and retreat into the forest for a life of contemplation and devotion to higher knowledge leading to liberation *(mokṣa)*. With the passage of time, however, the truths discerned at the forest retreats seeped into the marketplace and onto the battlefield. In the Upaniṣads we find kings seeking spiritual knowledge; in the *Bhagavad Gītā*, the warrior Arjuna gains the enlightened counsel of Krishna during a dialogue that has become perhaps the most famous conversation in the history of religious literature. Eventually, the quest for liberation spilled over into virtually all dimensions of Hindu life. The Purāṇic literature, in the form of popular stories of gods and warriors first told around 500 C.E., brought to the masses the lofty ideals previously privy only to the Brahmans and Buddhist monks. As Madeleine Biardeau has noted, "the purāṇas. . . opened the mind to the idea of accessibility of mokṣa to all." Citing various passages from the later sections of the *Mahābhārata*, she observes that this new, liberalized conception of liberation

> gave every svadharma [one's own societal duty] religious content and an access to ultimate salvation. The Brahmanic model was not lost sight of, but was generalized so as to fit all other categories of Hindu society, including sudras, women, and all impure castes. Once the ksatriya gained access to salvation through his specific and impure activities, the generalization became easy. Every sort of impurity could be sacralized and turned into svadharma. Nothing was outside the realm of ultimate values, though at the same time the status of the Brahmans remains unimpaired.[9]

This development in the history of the Indian conception of liberation opened the way for religious practice based more on accomplishment than on birth, and thereby included masses who had previously been disenfranchised from the brahmanical model. In the transition from the exclusively Brahman access to the highest truth to its more generalized formulation by the time of the medieval period, certain aspects of practice became emphasized that allowed for involvement in the world rather than requiring retreat to the forest for the obtainment of spiritual knowledge.

One of the central developments was the increased emphasis put upon the ability of human effort to change the script of one's karmic constitution.[10]

The task of the present work is to textually and historically trace the development of the concept that action can be conducted in such a manner as to allow one to shape his or her world and ultimately to advance towards liberation. The next chapter will examine the Vedic approach to action; as we will see, action is linked in the *Ṛg Veda* to sacrifice and creative power. Through sacrificial action, desired goals are fulfilled, and chaos is overcome. At a later time, the Upaniṣads and Sāṃkhya introduce the idea that beyond the fulfillment of mundane desires a higher truth in the form of the "unseen seer" *(ātman* or *puruṣa)* can be found. However, the quest for this self requires that the aspirant understand the creative process of action; the adept gains control over both the manifest world and the practices that leads to its dissolution. With this skill comes freedom in action, as we will see in the analogy of the potter's wheel at the conclusion of chapter two.

The later Upaniṣads and the *Yoga Sūtra*, examined in chapter three, regard the mind as the key to unlocking the mysteries of action, worldly manifestation, and liberation. A knowledge is sought that delivers one from the bondage of compulsive action and allows for unhindered creativity. The "mind-only" traditions found in the *Laṅkāvatāra Sūtra* of Yogācāra Buddhism and the *Yogavāsiṣṭha* of later Hinduism, similarly regard the regulation of the mind through meditation as the key to liberation. Passages on mind-only from each text are translated and discussed.

In the fourth chapter, the cultivation of effort as the means to transform one's thinking and, subsequently, one's actions, is examined in epic literature. This voluntarist philosophy, which affirms action as an effective vehicle for purification, is discussed in light of chapters from the *Mahābhārata* and the *Yogavāsiṣṭha* wherein this perspective on action is first learned and then espoused by the sage Vasiṣṭha. Translations of these passages are given in the appendices. Vasiṣṭha's teachings, as we will see, advocate an approach to karma that allows for reconciliation of worldly activity with higher spiritual values in a manner similar to that mentioned above by Biardeau.

The final chapter focuses on the broader theological issues implied in Vasiṣṭha's voluntarism. Can the spiritual freedom attained by those skilled in meditation be used to benefit those still involved with worldly activities? Can the manifest be seen as having usefulness within the quest for release? Through the *Bhagavad Gītā*, positive answers to both these questions are found: by surrendering attachment and performing action in a selfless manner, one can become free from the binding influence of past karma.

This study examines neither the depths of suffering *(duḥkha)* nor the lofty heights of release *(nirvāṇa, mokṣa, kaivalyam,* etc.*)*. Rather, this work is concerned with the crossroads: the special gift of being human that allows for a connection to be made between the mundane and the unspeakable. In summary and in introduction to the chapters that follow, this study explores societal responsibility not as antithetical to human freedom but as a path of liberation that engages both action and creativity when performed without attachment. Through activity, the binding influences of the past are overcome and a new order, a new vision is brought forth, a way of life anchored in creativity rather than mired by past actions.

2

Action and Origins in the Vedas, the Upaniṣads, and the *Sāṃkhya Kārikā*

The Ṛg Veda

How a culture regards its origins, its creation, tells much about the expectations it holds for its inheritors. In the search for beginnings, the starting point for India is the *Ṛg Veda*, oldest of the translated Indian and Indo-European literary documents. Composed by invaders probably from the steppes of Central Asia, the *Ṛg Veda* offers praise to various gods, singing of a cattle-herding, nomadic, war-filled way of life. The hymns, dating from about 1750 or 1500 B.C. to 500 B.C., are part of an oral and aural tradition that continues in present-day Hinduism. The Vedic creation stories tell of the world and gods and humans produced by sacrifice, and of sacrifices that must repeatedly be performed in order to ensure the continuity of culture.

In contrast to the Western traditions, there is no central creator god in the Vedic and Upaniṣadic traditions. Nor is there one coherent story. There is a repetition of creative themes revolving around sacrifice, and a virtual panoply of gods that serve as foci for multiple sacrifices. Indra, analogous to the Nordic Thor, institutes order and serves as a protector and warrior. Varuṇa, the god of fulness and swelling, brings happiness and peace. Agni, the god of fire, makes sacrifice possible. A creation story, gathered from various Vedic hymns, is summarized as follows:

> Before any creation emerges, there is only the primal waters, representing a totality of possibilities, enclosed and held back by the dragon Vṛtra. Goodness, personified by the god Varuṇa, strives for release from the dragon's constraint but is unsuccessful. But in addition to Vṛtra and Varuṇa there is a third god, the fashioner, Tvaṣṭṛ, who has created heaven and earth. From the union of heaven and earth is born the warrior Indra who, by drinking Soma, the elixir of the immortals, expands and becomes strong. Indra first forces apart heaven and earth; then he slays Vṛtra, the dragon who holds back the waters. Indra thus opens the realm of possibilities, releases the flow of life, and separates Existence *(sat)* from Non-Existence *(asat)*. Once this has been accomplished, Varuṇa and the other gods create order; to them sacrifices are performed and the continuity of human culture *(ṛta)* is maintained.[1]

This hybrid myth, threads of which appear throughout the text, does not specify creation as taking place through the agency of a supreme being, nor does it begin at a particular point in time nor, once set in motion, does it necessarily continue. The *Ṛg Veda* again and again finds Indra slaying the dragon. Existence again and again rises from Non-Existence. The gods are born only afterwards, and are kept alive only through sacrifice performed by men and women. The *Hymn of Creation* (X.129) states:

> Who really knows? Who will here proclaim it?
> When was it produced? Whence is this creation?
> The gods came afterwards, with the creation
> of the universe.
> Who then knows whence it has arisen?[2]

The process of creation happens with the birth of each new circumstance, like the arising of a new melody. The world has no fixed beginning but is in a state of flux, ready to take form with the initiation of sacrifice.

The *Ṛg Veda* is saturated with crisis and strife: the Vedic people did not reside in cultural unity but were continually confronted with opposition and difficulty. Antonio deNicolás has developed an interpretation of Vedic literature that sees strife as an integral force in the shaping of this originary world view, a force that ultimately has led to an unparalleled tolerance of diverse points of view. Four languages are outlined that incorporate the creative process. The first, symbolized by the dragon Vṛtra, is chaos, utter possibility *(asat)*. From this, a fixed structure arises that organizes a coherent view *(sat)*. This fixity is then ruptured through sacrifice *(yajña)*, so that a totality of the movement of culture may be experienced. This fourth state, referred to as embodied vision *(ṛtadhiḥ)*, is a vision of totality that allows for continued movement and has as its cultural legacy given birth to the Indian tolerance of multiplicity. This process of moving from nonexistence to existence to sacrifice to total vision never ends: the Vedic world depends on its constant engagement. This movement has been explained as follows:

> We have *Vṛtra*, the dragon, and his cohort of ophidians, as the prototypes of the *Asat*, covering up the possibilities of cultural man, either through inaction or dogmatism. Heroes like Indra and a multitude of gods are the prototype of the multiple ontologies of the *Sat;* Agni, Varuṇa, Prajāpati [Lord of Creatures, to be mentioned later], etc., are the prototypes of sacrifice *(yajña);* while *Ṛta* embodies the totality of languages, activities, images, and in general, the total cultural movement that needs its own continuous sacrifice of particular perspectives so that the whole cultural body may remain totally alive. . .[3]

For the Vedic sage, there is no ultimate experience, only the surrender of perspective to allow for the emergence of new experience and renewed culture. Dogmatism or inactivity is the greatest impediment to human freedom and must be overcome through sacrifice.

The concept of sacrifice *(yajña)* is one of the most puzzling aspects of the Indian world view. In the English language, we speak of ourselves as "sacrificing" the best years of our life in order to raise our children or giving up something that we would clearly prefer to continue possessing. The mood of sacrifice is often one of discomfort accompanied by regret. In another usage, we might speak of animal sacrifice wherein a goat is slain to appease an unhappy god. In either case, there is a firm distinction between the performer of the sacrifice and the benefactor. The performance and intention of Vedic sacrifice substantially differs from the concept generally connoted by the term. The prime function of the sacrifice is to generate heat within the body of the performer. This heat, called *tapas,* arises out of action[4] and is generated when the thoughts and intentions of the sacrificer are totally absorbed into that which is the object of the sacrifice. The action required for this transformation to take place has been described by Charles Malamoud as "the vital impulse which carries a being to realize his desires, to bring about his designs, to translate into works his thoughts."[5] For instance, a circumstance may require that one become a great warrior; like Indra, the sacrificer might deem it necessary to slay a "dragon" such as inertia or dogmatism. Through the performance of ritual action *(karma) tapas* is generated that allows the sacrificer to take on the qualities of Indra and achieve the desired goal. The process unleashes a creative force that leads to cultural unity and revitalizing vision *(ṛta-dhiḥ).* Through the application of *tapas,* creative intention is cultivated that has the power to link the microcosmic world of the sacrificer with the macrocosm, giving him or her the power to determine and alter circumstances, to bring forth new worlds and new possibilities.[6] This sacrifice has as its objective a unity of the sacrificer with the powers represented in what is sacrificed to. The performance of creative action generates a specific world symbolized by one of the various gods in the Vedic pantheon. The god to whom one sacrifices will change as one's needs and desires change.

The practical advantage of this Vedic system of sacrifice is that it recognizes the unpredictability of human needs. The participants in the sacrifice responsibly and knowingly construct a world for themselves and others through the sacrifice, through the invocation of a world order by recitation of the chant. Never static or dogmatic, the *Ṛg Veda* offers a mode of creative action that is perpetually renewed, a model that influences contemporary Hindu perspectives on the continuity of life. Creation is intimately linked to the performance of sacrifice. Through the vital impulse of ritual action, the sacrificer gains access to a creative power that is simultaneously microcosmic and macrocosmic.

The Creation Story of the *Śatapatha Brāhmaṇa*

The *Śatapatha Brāhmaṇa*, an important work in the history of early Hindu texts, tells a story of creation which, similar to Vedic accounts, links the emergence of world order with the performance of *tapas*.[7] In the beginning was nonexistence *(asat)*, the realm of possibility, symbolized by seven primal seers *(ṛṣis)*. The seers are identified with the vital airs, which in turn are identified with Indra, the holder of power, the kindler of the sacrificer, the performer of *tapas*. This group of seven seers merge into one person *(puruṣa)*, who then transforms into Prajāpati, Lord of Creation, symbolized by fire *(agni)*. Through the *tapas* of Prajāpati, the cosmos emerges, first as the *brahman*, also referred to as the Veda. Prajāpati then issues forth water out of speech. From Prajāpati's union with water, an egg appears: the juice of the egg becomes a horse, an ass, a goat, and a tortoise; the shell becomes the earth. Then all merge again into water. Prajāpati again performs *tapas*, transforming water into foam, which then transforms into clay, mud, soil, and sand, gravel, rock, ore, gods, plants, and trees. Then Prajāpati desires to join with the earth. He does so and another egg is formed. The embryo of this earth-born egg becomes wind; the juice becomes birds and sunbeams; the shell becomes the sky. Having created the sky, he desires union with it, which is accomplished by means of the sun. Yet another egg is formed, which becomes the moon, the stars, and the eight directions. Prajāpati's desires continue and, through the performance of *tapas* and the engagement of his mind (*manas*), various classes of gods and mortal beings, the seasons, and the sacrifice are brought forth. The sacrifice becomes the human vehicle for emulating the creative powers of Prajāpati. Through each of Prajāpati's creative endeavors, three factors are present: desire, *tapas*, and mind.

The act of creation through this process may be read both as a cosmogonic myth and as a symbol of creative power in a person. In the above story, the elements and the world are generated through desire *(kāma)* and *tapas*. The generation of heat in sacrifice gives birth to new combinations, new states of being. Within Brahmanical Hinduism, this process became ritualized in the performance of sacrifices administered by the priestly class, a practice that continues to the present day. However, powers of Prajāpati are universal human abilities manifested through desire and the fulfillment of desire through intentional acts. The creative process is engaged through sacrifice. Desire and *tapas* allow Prajāpati to create; these also allow humans to bring forth desired realms. The universe is molded into being by the attention and devotion of the sacrificer. The sacrificer establishes the center of a creation; his desire (or the desires of those who have engaged him) and his power of *tapas* give birth to new worlds, new possibilities. This creative process is summarized in the *Śatapatha Brāhmaṇa* as follows: "A man is born into the world he has made."[8] These worlds, by nature of their dependent origination, bear no ultimacy; they arise only to fade away, just as the many eggs produced by Prājapati gave way to new manifestations. Another sacrifice is always around the corner, just as in the *Ṛg Veda* the dragon Vṛtra always needs to be slain. Hence, creation is a continual process, requiring constant attention and repeated rekindling.

Creation in the *Bṛhadāraṇyaka Upaniṣad*

The *Bṛhadāraṇyaka Upaniṣad*, perhaps the earliest Upaniṣadic text, tells several stories regarding origins. The first account (I:2) begins with Death, in space, desiring a self. First water appears, the foam of which solidifies into earth. On this earth, Death performs *tapas*, producing fire. He then divides himself into three parts: fire, sun, and wind. Various bodily parts transform into the regions of the world: the east is formed from his head, the west from his tail-bone, the north and south from his flanks, the sky from his back, the atmosphere from his belly, the earth from his chest. Out of desire, Death then creates the year, speech, the *Ṛg Veda*, the *Yajur Veda*, and the *Sāma Veda;* he creates sacrifices, humans, and cattle. The creation thus completed, Death again performs *tapas*. The vital breaths leave him and his body swells into the form of a horse. This cosmic horse, found also in the Vedic horse sacrifice *(aśva-medha)*, is no other than the entire universe:

> Om! Verily, the dawn is the head of the sacrificial horse; the sun, his eye; the wind, his breath; universal fire, his open mouth. The year is the body *(ātman)* of the sacrificial horse; the sky, his back; the atmosphere, his belly; the earth, the underpart of his belly; the quarters, his flanks; the intermediate quarters, his ribs; the seasons, his limbs; the months and half-months, his joints; days and nights, his feet; the stars, his bones; the clouds, his flesh. Sand is the food in the stomach; rivers are his entrails. His liver and lungs are the mountains; plants and trees, his hair. The east is his fore part; the west, his hind part. When he yawns, then it lightens. When he shakes himself, then it thunders. When he urinates, then it rains. Voice, indeed, is his voice (I:I).

The many parts of the sacrificial horse, equalling the entire universe, are identical with the parts of Prajāpati's body, which in turn is identical with the human body. The priest, as mediator between the human and cosmic body, enters into the creation process by performing sacrificial rituals. But this creation process is also accessible to the reader of the Upaniṣadic text, who enters into the sacrificial view: through creative imagination, the reader's body becomes the body of Prajāpati, the body of the sacrificial horse, the symbol of totality.

Another creation story in the *Bṛhadāraṇyaka* (I:4) explains how each of the various animals and types of humans arose. The account begins, as before, with a solitary being. This person *(ātman* or *puruṣa)* uttered the words "I am" *(aham asmi)*, thus giving birth to the word "I." However, this primal being was not the usual type of person, but was the shape of a man and woman intimately embraced, as in Aristophanes' description of primal man-woman in Plato's *Symposium*. In order to remedy the feeling of aloneness, the person fell into two parts: man and woman, thus creating the human race. The woman then transformed herself successively into a cow, a mare, a goat, and an ewe, and in each instance, the man transformed himself into the appropriate male of the species and copulated with the female until all pairs of animals were created. That first person *(puruṣa)* then realized: "I, indeed, am this creation, for I emitted it all from myself. . . . Indeed, whoever has this knowledge comes to be in that self-creation" (I:4:5).

The *Bṛhadāraṇyaka* emphasizes the creative power of self. "Whoever worships another divinity thinking 'he is one and I another,' he knows not" (I:4:10). As the basis of all creation, the self is the only imperishable: "The work of the one who worships the Self alone as his world does not perish, for out of that very Self he creates whatsoever he desires" (I:4:15). The following passage gives examples of what can be obtained through oneself:

> Now this Self, verily, is a world of all created things. Insofar as a man makes offerings and sacrifices, he becomes the world of the gods. Insofar as he learns [the Vedas], he becomes the world of the seers *(ṛṣi)*. Insofar as he offers libations to the fathers and desires offspring, he becomes the world of the fathers. Insofar as he gives lodging and food to men, he becomes the world of men. Insofar as he finds grass and water for animals, he becomes the world of animals. Insofar as beasts and birds, even to the ants, find a living in his houses, he becomes their world. Verily, as one would desire security for his own world, so all creatures wish security for him who has this knowledge (I:4:16).

By involving oneself in a particular activity, one comes to embody it, whether it be concerned with sacrificial matters, family concerns, or even animal welfare. Through the self, each of these worlds can be attended to and fulfilled.

The sixth chapter of the *Bṛhadāraṇyaka Upaniṣad* describes the process by which humans are created from the remains of prior bodies.[9] This involves a series of sacrificial rites regarding human birth as continuous with and dependent on ecological cycles. When a person is cremated, the subtle remains contained in the smoke are sacrificed into the heavens, giving rise to King Soma. King Soma is then sacrificed into the raincloud, giving rise to rain. Rain is then sacrificed, falls to the earth, and plants arise. Plants are sacrificed as food and eaten by men, causing semen to be generated. Semen is sacrificed in women, and a person *(puruṣa)* is conceived and born. Human reproduction is here identified with universal, watery, life-giving processes. The creation process is a never-ending cycle, self-perpetuating and hence ensuring the continuity of life. It is interesting to note that this account of the birth and rebirth process does not state or imply that the nature of one's actions will determine one's status in a later embodiment; the early Indian mind seemed to be primarily concerned with immediate results of actions.

The *Bṛhadāraṇyaka Upanisạd* contains the teachings of the sage Yājñavalkya, one of the seminal thinkers of Indian history. Yājñavalkya states that karma or action has a direct effect on present life, following the course of one's desire:

> According as one acts, according as one
> conducts himself, so does he become.
> The doer of good becomes good; of bad, evil. . . .
> As is his desire, such is his resolve;
> as is his resolve, such the action he performs;
> what action he performs, that he procures for himself (IV:4:5).

One's desires lead to the desired world; though deceptively simple, this insight into karma shows that one's mind actively structures the world that is experienced. Yājñavalkya continues, quoting an earlier verse:

> Where one's mind is attached — the inner self
> Goes thereto with action, being attached to it alone.

Obtaining the end of his action,
Whatever he does in this world,
He comes again from that world
To this world of action.
— So the man who desires (IV:4:6).

Having realized how the mundane world operates, Yājñavalkya urges one to see that the true self is beyond all action, and to rise above ideas of right and wrong, so that "What he has done and what he has not done do not affect him" (IV:4:22). Through this achievement, having seen that the self is "not this, not this" *(neti, neti)*, the self *(ātman)* is then seen in all things, making one free from evil, impurity, doubt, and fear.

In another section of the text (III:8), the sage Yājñavalkya discusses with his wife, Gārgī, the nature of existence and its basis in the self. Gārgī opens the conversation by asking her husband what lies above the sky and beneath the earth. Yājñavalkya replies that space is the foundation of earth and sky, and space itself is woven on the imperishable *(akṣara)*. This imperishable, defying all description, orders the universe. Yājñavalkya proclaims:

At the command of the Imperishable
the sun and moon stand apart. . .
the earth and sky stand apart. . .
the moments, the hours, the days,
the nights, the years stand apart. . .
some rivers flow from snowy mountains
to the east, others to the west (III:8:9).

This silent force, like the powers of Indra and Varuṇa in the Vedic texts, underlies all creation. But Yājñavalkya stresses the immanence of this power, stating that it cannot be found beyond the sky or under the earth, but is discerned through the realization of the basis of human consciousness. His formula for the imperishable epitomizes the Upaniṣadic concern for the unspeakable that has influenced virtually all later schools of thought:

The Imperishable is the unseen Seer,
the unheard Hearer, the unthought Thinker,
the ununderstood Understander (III:8:11).

The Imperishable, the cause of outward manifestations associated with time and space, in reality lies within the human order as the unreflective self. This self *(ātman* or *puruṣa)* is the *telos* of knowledge for the wise but, as we will see, requires constant vigilance and repeated sacrifice in order to be realized.

Though we have by no means exhausted the philosophical content of the *Bṛhadāraṇyaka Upaniṣad,* three themes dealing with creation have been explored. The first links creation with a primal sacrifice that is performed repeatedly to ensure the continuity of culture. Though originally in the form of a horse sacrifice *(aśva-medha)* the text implies that less elaborate sacrifices using visualization are equally efficacious, and reveals that the creation of "worlds" takes place through the active pursuit of desires. The second, more biological account, describes how the human body arises from water, linking man/woman with an ecological totality. The third account, articulated by Yājñavalkya, emphasizes that what is created is not the true purpose of life and that knowledge of the imperishable self is the highest knowledge to be obtained. Attachment to creation must be sacrificed in order for liberation to take place.

The Quest for Self in the *Chāndogya Upaniṣad*

The *Chāndogya Upaniṣad,* like the *Bṛhadāraṇyaka,* acknowledges that worlds are gained through desire. But, as the eighth chapter asserts, desire for the true self is higher than pursuing worldly things. The text states that by the mere power of conception *(saṃkalpa)* the desired result is obtained, whether it be the world of the fathers or that of the mothers, brothers, sisters or friends, or the world of perfume or garlands, food or drink, song or music, women or "whatever object" (VIII:2:1). For one who searches out and obtains food, song, women, etc., there is no release; although the desire is real *(satya kāma),* it is not desire for the "real" or true self (VIII:3:1). For those who have found the self through yearning desire for the real, "in all worlds there is freedom" (VIII:1:6). A story is then told, one of the best known passages in the Upaniṣads, wherein Indra, a god, and Virocana, a demon, seek out Prajāpati's instruction regarding the true nature of the self. It opens with a statement by Prajāpati regarding the goal to be achieved:

> The Self *(ātman)*, which is free from evil, ageless, deathless, sorrowless, hungerless, thirstless, whose desire is the Real, whose conception is the Real — that should be searched out, that one should desire to understand. All worlds and all desires are obtained by the one who has found out and who understands that Self (VIII:7:1).

Indra and Virocana, with offerings in hand, go to Prajāpati for instruction regarding the self. After both god and demon perform *tapas* for thirty-two years, Prajāpati reveals his first teaching: 'The physical body, well-adorned, is your true self." Virocana, satisfied and quite delighted, returns home to the demons to preach a new cult of self-indulgence. Indra, on the other hand, doubts the teaching, reasoning that the body is perishable and, hence, cannot be the true self. He returns to Prajāpati, who acknowledges the fallacy of his teaching but will say no more — Indra must perform *tapas* for another thirty-two years. After the required time passes, the second teaching is given: "He who moves about happy in a dream — he is the true self." Indra, at first elated, soon expresses disbelief: all dreams are not happy ones. If the self is eternal, it cannot be in dream. Prajāpati concurs, admitting that his statement is not complete. However, he demands thirty-two more years of Indra's life. The years pass and, finally, Prajāpati proclaims his third teaching: "When one is sound asleep, composed, serene, and knows no dream, that is the true self, the immortal, the fearless, the Brahman." Indra at first smiles, thinking the ultimate truth has been gained. But then he scratches his head and challenges his mentor: "If nothing can be perceived, how can the self be known?" In turn, Prajāpati smiles and says, "Yes, you have found the fault with this teaching as well. Stay with me for five more years. Then, Indra, you will receive the true teaching." After the five years, Prajāpati grants Indra a lengthy visit and instructs him as follows:

> Verily, there is no freedom from pleasure and pain for one who is in the body. As a workhorse is yoked in a wagon, so is this energy *(prāṇa)* yoked in this body.
>
> When the eye is directed toward space, that is the seeing witness *(cākṣuṣa puruṣa)*; the eye is but the instrument for sight. The one who says "Let me smell this" is the true self *(ātman)*; the nose is merely the instrument for smelling. The one who says "Let me say this" is the true self; the voice is only a vehicle.
>
> The one who knows "Let me think this" — that is the true self; the mind *(manas)* is the divine eye *(daiva cakṣu)*. That one, with the divine eye, the mind, sees desires here, and experiences enjoyment.
>
> Those gods who are in the Brahmā world reverence that Self. Therefore all worlds and all desires have been appropriated by them. He obtains all worlds and all desires who has found out and who understands that Self *(ātman)* (VIII:12).

While the *Bṛhadāraṇyaka* emphasizes the unspeakable aspect of the self, the *Chāndogya* extols the self as the context for the obtainment of worlds, and the fulfillment of desires. In both instances, the self is not found in what is seen, but in the one who sees: detachment from the objects of the senses is a prerequisite to vision of the self.

Furthermore, the *Chāndogya* is careful to point out the necessity of the quest for knowledge. Yājñavalkya pronounced his wisdom openly to his wife Gārgī and to King Janaka. In contrast, Prajāpati taught that the essence of life is to be found in the systematic and careful analysis of the self under the tutelage of a qualified teacher. In order to obtain knowledge, Indra had to endure 101 years of waiting before he learned to live his life through the senses with the understanding that the senses are mere tools, following the bidding of an unseen master. The apprenticeship is part of another dimension of Indian thought wherein free and creative living does not spontaneously arise as in Vedic times but must be cultivated through training under a qualified teacher.

Creation and Dissolution in Sāṃkhya

The story of Indra's tutelage by Prajāpati, the Lord of Creation, establishes the need for the cultivation of a specialized form of human knowledge *(jñāna)*. This is not a knowledge of phenomena, but a knowledge of the self that is beyond change, described in the *Bhagavad Gītā* as "not burned by fire, not wetted by water, untouched by wind; eternal, all pervading, unmoving, unmanifest, unchanging" (II:24-25). This self, referred to as *ātman* or *puruṣa*, is the foundation and ending point for almost every system of Indian thought. Whereas instruction regarding this self is given in stories and panegyric in Upaniṣadic literature, later traditions developed elaborate philosophical systems to communicate the experience of this self and the means by which it could be attained. One such system is Sāṃkhya, which explains not only how creation emerges but how the creative process can be arrested so that liberation may be obtained. It describes the emergence of the world as a process of unfoldment intimately linked with human psychology. However, unlike the Vedic texts, it does not recommend that one fulfill one's desires. Rather, like the *Chāndogya Upaniṣad*, it first asks its readers to understand how desires are made manifest. But then it asks that one learn to discriminate between *prakṛti*, the realm of unending change through which desires are fulfilled, and *puruṣa*, one's true self, which is beyond all predication and flux and, hence, not subject to the suffering that arises when desire and expectations are thwarted. Herein a new dimension of Indian philosophy is emphasized, one that has profound ramifications for Hindu theories of action. As opposed to calling for actions to be undertaken for the satisfaction of desires, the Sāṃkhya system calls for a neutralization of action so that liberation can be experienced. A type of action is propounded in Sāṃkhya that causes one to progressively withdraw from attachment to the manifest world and refocus one's awareness on the distinctions between the manifest, the unmanifest, and the unseen witness, the forever free experience of *puruṣa*. Processes of mind and the cultivation of this specialized knowledge *(jñāna)* play a pivotal role in Sāṃkhya. In the following section, major aspects of this system will be highlighted that pertain to the mind, its relationship to action, and the implications of action in the quest for liberation.

Sāṃkhya is regarded as one of the six main schools *(darśana)* of orthodox Hindu thought. Although Sāṃkhya terminology pervades the *Śvetāśvatāra* and *Maitri Upaniṣads* and is used extensively in the *Mahābhārata* and the Purāṇas, its formal expression is found in a different genre of text, the *Sāṃkhya Kārikā* of Īśvarakṛṣṇa, probably written in the third century C.E. Unlike the picturesque Vedic and Upaniṣadic literature, the *Sāṃkhya Kārikā* is terse and precise, in the classical tradition of stringing together epigrammatic philosophical statements. The entire Sāṃkhya system is contained in just seventy-two short verses, which have provided a rich ground for an extensive commentarial tradition.[10] The system is simultaneously instructive and prescriptive, saying of itself that reflection on its contents leads to liberative knowledge.

Creation of the manifest world in the Sāṃkhya system does not begin with sacrifice prompted by desire. Rather, the emergence of the world is attributed to the coming together *(saṃyoga)* of *puruṣa,* the unchanging witness or consciousness, and *prakṛti,* the ever-changing domain of things wherein particularities are delineated and mundane life proceeds. From *prakṛti* is said to unfold twenty-three other *tattvas* (literally, "that-nesses"), each of which is composed of varying degrees of three constituents or strands *(guṇa):* heaviness *(tamas),* passion *(rajas),* and lightness *(sattva). Prakṛti* remains in an unmanifested state until it is enlivened by consciousness *(puruṣa).* As long as consciousness is not present, the world remains unmanifest: there is no production of the other twenty-three *tattvas* and, hence, no mind and no objects. Only when *puruṣa* and *prakṛti* come together can the mind begin to operate and the world be known. Hence, rather than presenting a mythological or allegorical account of how creation takes place, the Sāṃkhya system as we will see, gives a detailed descriptive phenomenology of perceptual processes, their interaction with the world, and the relationship of the senses and the world with pure consciousness.

The first manifestation of *prakṛti* to arise from her association with *puruṣa* is intellect *(buddhi)*, closely followed by sense-of-self *(ahaṃkāra)* and the perceptive vehicle or mind *(manas)*. These three manifestations *(tattvas)*, primarily composed of lightness *(sattva)*, determine how the rest of the world will be perceived. Through the combined qualities of lightness and passion *(rajas)*, the five sense organs and the five organs of action are generated. These ten (eye, ear, nose, tongue, skin; voice, hands, feet, and the respective organs of reproduction and excretion) constitute the basis for human corporeality. Concurrently, passion mixes with heaviness *(tamas)* to bring forth out of *prakṛti* the five subtle elements (sound, touch, form, taste, smell), which are then said to generate the five gross elements (space, wind, fire, water, earth). The earth is the last manifestation of reality to take place in this creation story. To recapitulate, the process begins when *prakṛti*, the unconscious, meets up with *puruṣa*, the conscious. Then, she begins to spin out her creation, starting first with mind, followed by sense and action organs. Only after these have emerged does the physical domain appear. (See figure one.)

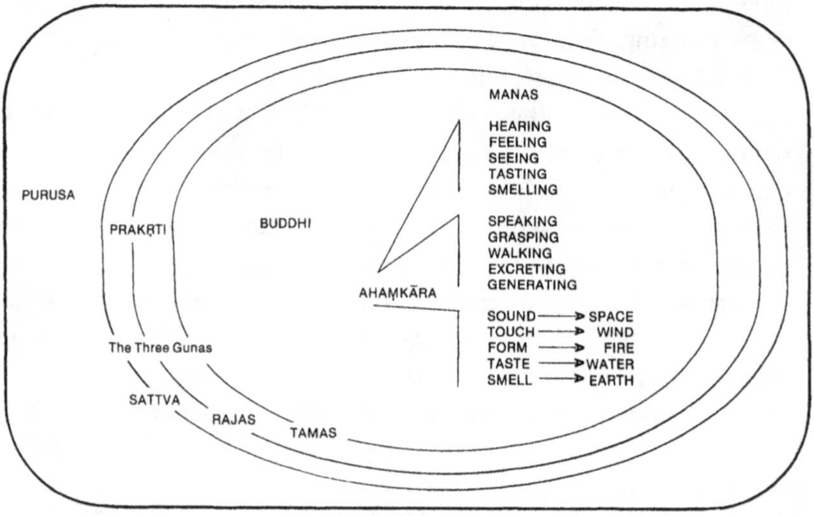

FIGURE ONE: The 25 tattvas of the Sāṃkhya System

Sāṃkhya accounts for all aspects of creation, both the person and the physical world, as being comprised of the twenty-four *tattvas* cited above. The emergence of the world follows and depends upon the dispositions of the mind and body. Being composed of *prakṛti*, the mind (including the sense of self-image), the body, and the physical world are in a state of perpetual flux. Just as the Hindu cyclic theory of time predicts successive eras that arise and disappear, the world as manifested by *prakṛti* and experienced by *puruṣa* is assumed to be similarly vulnerable to ultimate demise. For the ordinary person this comes with death, and is generally feared. Conversely, for the practitioner of Sāṃkhya, the imminent demise of the manifestations of *prakṛti* is not regarded as a terrible fate; rather, it is actively sought out as a state of blessedness, a condition in which one's true nature as pure consciousness may be discerned. By identifying with consciousness rather than the manifestations of *prakṛti*, a state of aloneness *(kaivalyam)* is attained that frees one from the bondage of experience. However, as we will see, the practice of Sāṃkhya does not require the actual neurological disengagement from the phenomenal world through dying, but demands the cultivation of an understanding that leads to the discernment of one's authentic noninvolvement with the changes inherent in being human.

The attainment of liberation in the Sāṃkhya system requires that one thoroughly comprehend both the process of manifestation and its reverse. The former is the basic human condition; the latter involves a close examination of how perception works, which, it is to be hoped, will lead to an enlightened state of discernment. The key to this investigation is the intellect *(buddhi)*, the first product to issue from *prakṛti* when she associates with *puruṣa*. According to the *Sāṃkhya Kārikā*, intellect serves as the conduit that allows the data collected by *prakṛti* to be presented to *puruṣa*. However, when this occurs, the intellect, although a product of *prakṛti* and, hence, by definition unconscious, appears to be conscious. Being mistaken for *puruṣa*, it causes actions to be attributed to consciousness that in reality is forever inactive. When this happens, the sense of self *(ahaṃkāra)* mistakenly claims responsibility for and authority over all acts of consciousness, thus ignoring the fact that the person who says "I know" is merely a product of *prakṛti* and is incapable of knowing anything without consciousness. It becomes impossible to distinguish the pure, undefiled, neutral witness *(puruṣa)* from the "I-maker" *(ahaṃkāra)*, the temporally bound aspect of *prakṛti* that lays claim to the manifest. Access to the world is limited to and defined by this all-pervasive, I-centered interpretation, which is subject to change and, hence, continually vascillates between experiences of and identification with pleasure and pain. Life thus lived is an unending repetition of bitter and sweet, as long as the intellect remains confused as to its true nature. Furthermore, the undisciplined intellect, in addition to its fundamental confusion, is laden with the impressions of past action. These inclinations, accumulated during prior experience, determine the outlook and orientation of the sense of self; this in turn influences the constitution of one's corporeality and thence the perception of the world. As long as the intellect remains confused and sullied by the influence of previous karma, the world as generated leads to repeated pain and delusion.

In order to extricate oneself from the net of mistaken identity and to overcome negative prior actions, the *Sāṃkhya Kārikā* offers a thorough analysis of the intellect, an understanding of which serves as an excellent introduction to later philosophical trends in India that emphasize the primacy of mind and the need for its purification. In Sāṃkhya, the intellect has the possibility of learning what it is not and thereby the capability of releasing *prakṛti* from her ignorance. In a sense, the intellect is the most important aspect of being human. Consequently, the *Sāṃkhya Kārikā* contains several verses that discuss intellect and divide it into *bhāvas*. This Sanskrit term, which will be left untranslated, literally means "state of being" and is derived from the verbal root *bhū*, which is cognate with the English verb "be." The *bhāvas* may also be considered as illustrative of specific modes of action. Two groupings of *bhāvas* are cited by Īśvarakṛṣṇa. The first, an eightfold analysis, outlines the means by which the intellect may be elevated to the point of being able to discriminate between the changes of *prakṛti* and the unchanging witness or *puruṣa;* this analysis will be examined in detail. The second grouping details fifty forms of delusion that will not be discussed in the present work.

The eight *bhāvas* fall into two syzygetic groups, one light *(sattvika)*, the other dark *(tamasika)*. Virtue *(dharma)*, knowledge *(jñāna)*, nonattachment *(virāga)*, and power *(aiśvarya)* constitute its light aspect; the dark aspect is comprised of four *bhāvas* opposite to those listed above: nonvirtue *(adharma)*, ignorance *(ajñāna)*, attachment *(rāga)*, and weakness *(anaiśvarya)*. (See figure two.)

sattvika:	*tamasika:*
Virtue - *dharma*	Nonvirtue - *adharma*
Knowledge - *jñāna*	Ignorance - *ajñāna*
Nonattachment - *virāga*	Attachment - *rāga*
Power - *aiśvarya*	Weakness - *anaiśvarya*

Chart Two: The Bhāvas of Buddhi

These modes or states of being pervade and shape the body that is then generated, including one's sense of self, its corresponding effect on one's perception of the world, and the path of action subsequently pursued. If the intellect finds its predominant expression in sloth and inability to succeed *(anaiśvarya)*, that person is said to be lazy, and his or her attitude is most likely to be that "the world is against me;" his or her actions would prove ineffectual. On the other hand, when vigor and positive thinking prevail, as would be the case for someone established in the power *(aiśvarya) bhāva*, success in action undoubtedly follows. Similarly, fixity in the attachment *bhāva* results in the constant pursuit of desire, resulting inevitably with periodic disappointment; nonattachment brings a state of contentment. Knowledge is said to bring liberation, and will be discussed in more detail below. Ignorance leads to actions of continued bondage. Virtue allows one to ascend to happier states; nonvirtue results in descent into activities associated with lower states of existence.

Each of the *bhāvas* is said to arise from one of two causes. The first cause listed by Īśvarakṛṣṇa states that the *bhāvas* are innate with each person. The second explanation for their arising indicates that the pattern of *bhāvas* can be acquired through human effort. If one is interested in becoming particularly lustful, this can be accomplished through the cultivation of nonvirtue and attachment. However, it is much more desirable to develop *bhāvas* that lead one out of confusion and into actions stemming from knowledge that is pure and liberating. This, in fact, is the telos of the Sāṃkhya system: to utilize human effort to bring about the *bhāva* of knowledge. The first step in this process is to see the functions and elements of existence as a system of interacting fields rather than as discrete objects and individual persons. Without referencing all phenomena to the sense of self, freedom is gained. The witness loses interest in the dance of *prakṛti* and is no longer lost in misidentification. Just as Prajāpati admonished Indra in the *Chāndogya Upaniṣad* to cultivate desire for the real as preferable to lower desires, the Sāṃkhya system calls for the distancing from desire through the cultivation of knowledge. The intellect plays a pivotal role in this process. If purified and established in knowledge, access to pure consciousness is gained. If not, one remains prey to the pain of misidentification, the taking on of limited identity and the unending difficulties thereby implicated. When the intellect becomes purified through knowledge and directed away from the manifest domain of *prakṛti*, then liberation is possible.

Of the intellect's eight *bhāvas*, knowledge *(jñāna)* holds the most elevated position, the key to liberation through which the distinctness of *puruṣa* from *prakṛti* is discerned. *Sāṃkhya Kārikā*, verse 63, states:

> It is by the seven forms (of *bhāvas*)
> that *prakṛti* binds herself for herself.
> And indeed, for the sake of *puruṣa*,
> she frees herself by means of one (knowledge).

Through the application of knowledge, cultivated and nurtured by contemplation on the process by which *prakṛti* creates the world and then mistakes an aspect of herself to be consciousness, the *puruṣa* is seen to have always been free of identity with the world of action. Hence, the experience of liberation is described by Īśvarakṛṣṇa as follows:

> Thus, from the analysis of the constituents [of *prakṛti*],
> arises the knowledge 'I am not, nothing is mine,
> I do not exist.' [This knowledge] is all-encompassing,
> free from error, pure, and final [67].

The intellect has been awakened to its mistake; the cultivation of knowledge has resulted in the cessation of the conception of self which sets itself up as the candidate for suffering. All such action is seen to be merely a manifestation of *prakṛti*, while *puruṣa*, one's authentic identity, remains eternally unaffected, unattached. At these moments of insight, *prakṛti* desists, no longer compelled to continue her dance. However, this experience does not necessarily cancel the possibility that *prakṛti* will return; the hiatus from her dance may only be temporary, as indicated in verse 68:

> The body, because of the force of past impressions,
> continues, like a potter's wheel.

As in the *Ṛg Veda*, the sacrifice does not cease; experiences of insight must be cultivated and repeated. Not until death is an eternal and absolute isolation *(kaivalyam)* from *prakṛti* attained.

In summary, one's thoughts and actions are seen in Sāṃkhya to play a vital role in the structure of the intellect and the subsequent apprehension of the world. Two groups of *bhāvas* constitute the intellect, one pure, the other impure. Action in accordance with either yields a predictable result. Through the cultivation of knowledge liberation can be experienced. This does not happen naturally, or by chance, or by luck. Only through the active pursuit of knowledge does impurity exhaust itself. This requires firm resolve, a voluntarism of the highest order wherein the very process of determining the world is brought into consciousness and directed to the goal of liberation.

In the Sāṃkhya system, the burden of reality falls upon the person. As Gerald Larson has written, "the world is not understood in itself apart from the fact of human existence. In a sense, then, the world is uniquely human."[11] The entire world process is inseparable from a man or woman's engagement of it.

With this "humanization" of the world comes a tremendous responsibility: bondage and liberation lie in each person's grasp, dependent on one's past history and current resolve. Life is conceived of as an interplay of human emotions, thoughts, and actions, a drama where the manifestations of *prakṛti* are determined by the *bhāvas* and, with practice, the *bhāvas* are held in control by knowledge *(jñāna)*. The *puruṣa* remains untouched, witnessing the ever-changing stage that *prakṛti* both creates and adorns. Inherent in the image of *prakṛti* as dancer is a sense that life is a beautiful event, to be encountered, appreciated, and finally transcended.

The potter's wheel, mentioned by Īśvarakṛṣṇa to explain how life continues after enlightenment, also provides an excellent analogy for understanding Sāṃkhya's philosophy of freedom through detachment in action. A potter creates dishes, bowls, and other utensils for use in everyday life. All of the elements are used: the earthen clay, water, heat produced from friction, air for drying, with space being filled by each. The first task for the potter is to center all the elements and confine the clay on the rotating wheel. In order for this to take place, the mind has to be stilled. The hands do the work; if a thought enters such as "I am going to make a perfect pot," the process is ruined and the pot is knocked off center. Hence, a steady detachment must be maintained: the action is performed, but the doer does not claim its fruits. Sitting above the spinning wheel, distanced and yet intimately involved, the witness silently watches the pot grow and take shape. There is reciprocity between the stillness and the activity. As in the yoga of action, the two modes work together for the creation of a new order. This skill in action, taken beyond the metaphor of the potter's wheel, liberates a person to move through life using what is needed but avoiding the pitfalls and broken dreams inherent in attachment. When the mind is filled with thoughts, it becomes impossible to move unencumbered; when the mind is pacified, the unity that results fosters true creativity.

In the Vedic texts studied earlier, we have seen how desire and *tapas*, arising from action, give birth to the sacrificial order. The sacrifice in turn maintains the world: the one who conceives of and procures desires reigns over his or her circumstances. Through the active pursuit of a goal, that desire is fulfilled. Sāṃkhya emphasizes knowledge rather than fulfillment, but the process similarly hinges on human effort. In the Vedic hymns, the sacrificer brings forth his or her own world and then works at maintaining it. In the Prajāpati story, the final enlightenment comes through the active embrace of the senses with simultaneous recognition of the cognizer. In Sāṃkhya, the knowledge leading to liberation begins with constant observation of *prakṛti* as she becomes manifest in the mind, body, and world. In each of these systems, the person is regarded as an integral whole, with desire, thought, deed, and body in unity. Self-conscious identity, the locus of ignorance and discomfort, must be transcended in order for the creative, sacrificial process to unfold and the silent, unseen witness to be realized. The *Sāṃkhya Kārikā* calls for action that does not aim at obtaining things but has knowledge as its goal. This knowledge transforms one's entire being, moving one away from actions rooted in suffering and toward liberation.

3

Primacy of Mind According to the Upaniṣads, the *Yoga* and *Laṅkāvatāra Sūtras*, and the *Yogavāsiṣṭha*

The mind as interpreted in the Cartesian model provides us with packets of facts about a preexisting external world and allows us to make well-informed, rational choices as we move through life. The existence of the world is presupposed; the mind's function is to provide clear and distinct representations of the world. In the classical Indian model, mind takes on a more creative dimension. In our discussion of Sāṃkhya we saw a threefold analysis of mental processes: (1) the mind *(manas)*, which functions as a conveyor of information; (2) a locus of self-identity *(ahaṃkāra)*; and (3) the intellect *(buddhi)*, a higher faculty that determines overall outlook and intentionality. The organizer, providing the frame for all these processes, is pure consciousness *(puruṣa)* that, though present at every moment, remains unseen and inactive.[1] In conventional states of being, *puruṣa* is covered over by the dominance of the mental functions mentioned above that embed in the individual the notion that the world is a given, static entity in opposition to one's conception of self. The first chapter of the *Bhagavad Gītā* illustrates the limitations of this mode when the warrior Arjuna, confronted with a crisis, is utterly unable to move due to his staunch adherence to past memories and expectations, his attachment to self and other.

Conventional consciousness takes for granted the reality and inherent value of externality. Sāṃkhya, however, undercuts the fixity of the world and brings into question both objectivity and subjectivity. Through the practice of knowledge *(jñāna)*, the reifying process of the mind can be reversed; the world, figuratively speaking, can be turned inside out. The emergence of things takes place through the coming together of witness and activity, *puruṣa* and *prakṛti*, and one gets swept away in an endless stream of thoughts and action. However, this can be brought into check by the practice of yoga in which the mind no longer binds one through its cognitive obsessions but is used as a tool, either spinning out a world when needed or dwelling in a state of meditative awareness. Hence, one gains access to both creativity and dissolution.

This philosophy of mind is not idealism in the sense that each mind creates reality. Such a literal reading fails to take into account the interplay and interdependency of *puruṣa* and *prakṛti*. Indian philosophy consistently posits a twofold reality, with one aspect constantly in flux, subject to the laws of cause and effect, the other aspect uninvolved, pure, and stainless. Human creativity lies in the unity of and distinction between these reciprocal dimensions; the mind becomes the tool used to cultivate life and the worlds in which one lives.

Mind in the Upaniṣads

The Indian view of the creative powers of the mind is found in both the early and later Upaniṣads. For instance, the *Chāndogya* states that "one should reverence the mind as Brahman."[2] The *Taittirīya* says "truly, indeed, beings are born from mind, when born they live by mind, on deceasing they enter into mind."[3] In the *Aitareya Upaniṣad*, "all this" (the world) is said to be guided by and cased on intelligence *(prajñāna)*.[4] The *Kauṣītaki* states that when intelligence is applied to any faculty, a totality is experienced; all elements *(bhūta)* depend upon the mind:

> With intelligence *(prajñā)* having mounted on
> speech, with speech one obtains all names. . .
> on breath, all odors. . .
> on the eye, all forms. . .
> on the ear, all sounds. . .
> on the tongue, all tastes. . .
> on the two hands, all works. . .
> on the body, pleasure and pain. . .
> on the generative organ, bliss, delight, and procreation. . .
> on the two feet, all goings. . .
> on the mind *(manas)*, all thoughts. . . .
> For truly, if there were no elements of being,
> there would be no elements of intelligence.
> Verily, if there were no elements of intelligence
> there would be no elements of being.
> For truly, from either alone,
> no appearance whatsoever would be effected.[5]

From this passage it is clear that the mind does not create out of nothing; the Upaniṣads do not advance an unsophisticated idealism. Rather, the important role of the mind in giving access to the world is emphasized, exposing a complementarity between the perceived and the means of perception. Without mind, no world could be known nor could any action be accomplished.

The *Maitri Upaniṣad* articulates the relationship between mind and spiritual liberation. The mind in its conventional state is sedimented with various impurities that obscure its fundamental power. A person at this level of understanding is a victim of circumstance, caught in repeated pain and delusion. However, when the power of mind is known, then one becomes freed from compulsive action. The text states that worldly existence is generated by thought:

Saṃsāra is just one's thought;
With effort then he should cleanse it.
What is one's thought that he becomes;
This is the eternal mystery.[6]

This cleansing process involves both thought and action and requires a restructuring of the desire that leads to action:

By tranquility of thought,
one destroys both good and evil deeds *(karman).*
The mind is said to be twofold: pure and impure.
Impure—by union with desire;
Pure—from desire completely free!
The mind, in truth, is for mankind
The means of bondage and release.
If bound to objects, bondage follows;
From objects free—that is called release![7]

Release involves a transformation so that the mind no longer becomes attached to the objects of sense due to compulsive past influences. When the senses are drawn inward, purification takes place, the mind is stilled, and *saṃsāra* is overcome.

THE TRANSFORMATION OF MIND *(Citta)* IN THE *Yoga Sūtra*

Both the Upaniṣads and the *Sāṃkhya Kārikā* affirm that the mind determines the nature of action and, hence, one's relationship with the world. It is not until the *Yoga Sūtra*, however, that we find the development of a highly sophisticated system for accomplishing the purification of mind. Classical Yoga, as presented by Patañjali and commented upon by Vyāsa, postdates the Upaniṣads and relies heavily upon the speculations of Sāṃkhya. It differs from each in its programmatic attempt to catalogue a plethora of techniques designed for recognizing the power of the mind and bringing it under control through regulation of actions and meditation. In this regard, it takes the Sāṃkhyan conception of mind one step further. Whereas Sāṃkhya emphasizes the importance of intellect in the process of worldly manifestation, Yoga first itemizes the shapes that the mind assumes when left to its own karmically influenced devices and then lists various practices, including meditation, that can be undertaken to free one from the afflictions that normally accrue as the result of actions pursued by the unbridled mind.

The *Yoga Sūtra* of Patañjali (ca. 200 C.E.)[8] combines the world-relies-on-thought threads of the Upaniṣads with the Sāṃkhyan quest for liberation. The Upaniṣads praise the powers of mind in various passages, as we have seen. Sāṃkhya gives a highly detailed analysis of the intellect and its many *bhāvas*. The *Yoga Sūtra,* without repeating the various Sāṃkhyan classifications, briefly states the various shapes taken by the mind in the process of perceiving the world and explicates various actions by which these may be brought under control. The philosophical position regarding ignorance and mistaken identity parallels that found in Sāṃkhya, but the *Yoga Sūtra* goes into far greater detail in explaining techniques by which the world of change may be abrogated and the true self revealed. The *Sāṃkhya Kārikā* essentially prescribes one practice only: the cultivation of knowledge. In contrast, Patañjali offers in excess of twenty discrete practices that can be undertaken to achieve yoga, the state in which the true self *(ātman* or *puruṣa)* is allowed to shine forth.

The cornerstone of yogic technique is the control of mind *(citta),* as stated in the second *sūtra:* "Yoga is the cessation of fluctuations in the mind."[9] The term *citta,* which will be translated here as mind, refers to what in Sāṃkhya corresponds to the first three manifested aspects of *prakṛti:* the intellect *(buddhi),* the sense of self *(ahaṃkāra),* and the perceptual faculty *(manas).* The mind is also the receptacle for the effects of karma, the residue *(saṃskāra)* left by action that forms habit patterns *(vāsanā).* The functioning of the mind takes place through fluctuations *(vṛtti)* that give form to perceptions, thoughts, emotions, and so forth. Five fluctuations are listed and described in the first section of the *Yoga Sūtra* (I:5–11). The first is valid cognition *(pramāṇa),* which allows for the perception of something that is fully manifested. Such experience is verified via one of three avenues: direct perception *(pratyakṣa),* inference *(anumāna),* and credible verbal account *(āgama).* Any perception of plants, animals, buildings, people, and so forth, whether by direct experience, inference, or testimony, belongs to this first class of fluctuation. The four other types of fluctuation explain other ways in which the mind operates. The second is error *(viparyaya)*, when a thought does not correspond with reality. The third, imagination *(vikalpa)*, involves a notion, not necessarily an error, which does not correspond to an object, but may in fact serve a useful function. Examples would be metaphor and simile in poetry. In states of meditation, imagination is important for the development of a strong mind. The fourth mind state is sleep *(nidrā)*, defined as the predominance of the intention of non-being *(abhāva)*. The last fluctuation listed is memory *(smṛti)*. In memory, contents of a previous experience are returned to consciousness via thought, although there is no longer any corresponding structure on the gross level.

These five states — valid cognition, error, imagination, sleep, and memory — comprise the normal range of human transaction, including things as directly perceived; thoughts, whether remembered, imagined, or false; and sleep. Each of these states is linked directly to a subjective appropriator, an "I" that claims the experience. In *Yoga Sūtra* IV:4, we find that "states of awareness (in particularized form) arise from the sense-of-I *(asmitā)* exclusively." That is, the perceptions of discrete objects or thoughts as described above arise from the sense of self *(ahaṃkāra)*. When this happens, the "higher" self, the noncreative witness *(ātman* or *puruṣa)* is blended into the seen. The result is the emergence or the evolution *(sarga)* of the *that*, the reification and solidification of the world in the form of the mind's fluctuations. This movement, the perception of things, thoughts, or sleep as appropriated by limited self-consciousness, constitutes conventional experience.

In the Yoga tradition, unlike Vedānta, the reality of the mind and its fluctuations is not denied. However, what in common usage are referred to as things *(vastu)* are seen in the yogic system as fluctuations stemming from the sense-of-I. The process of cultural conditioning, including the acquisition of appropriate names for certain fluctuations, establishes how the world is to be experienced and engaged. Once this educational process has been embedded, including culturally transmitted attitudes and prejudices, it becomes immovable, or very nearly so. One's perspective on life is restricted to a limited language of things and how the sense-of-self relates to those things. In such conventional consciousness, life is spent in the unending generation of essentially the same patterns; like the bar in a ripple tank, it continually emanates a surface of interfering waves and obscures the background of still water.

The unenlightened mind, due to prior sedimentation accumulated during action, is fraught with afflictions *(kleśa)* that in turn determine the course of one's actions. These are said to be five in number, and are listed in *Sūtra* II:3 as ignorance, sense-of-I, attachment, aversion, and clinging to life.[10] The root of each of these is ignorance *(avidyā)*, which is said to be taking the non-eternal to be eternal, the impure to be pure, discomfort to be pleasure, and the non-self to be the self.[11] As long as ignorance prevails, karma remains fraught with affliction. Recalling our introductory statements in chapter one, it is stated in the *Yoga Sūtra* that as long as afflictions remain at the root of action, the residue will continue to produce the three consequences of birth, span of life, and experience. Due to virtue or lack thereof, these will be either pleasurable or painful.[12] For the one who has gained Yogic wisdom, however, everything in the world of manifestation is seen to involve suffering:

> To the one with discriminative understanding,
> all is suffering by reason of the suffering
> caused by past impressions and their transformations,
> and due to the conflict in the fluctuations and the
> constituents *(guṇas)* [of *prakṛti*].[13]

Because the realm of *prakṛti* is in a state of continual flux it can produce no lasting satisfaction. Attachment to any one of these fleeting forms leads to disappointment and suffering.

Although the Yoga system has no qualms about expressing the shortcomings of mundane existence, it does not stop with existential despair. Patañjali asserts that there is a means to overcome attachment to the fluctuations of the mind and thereby achieve liberation from afflicted action. He states that "the fluctuations are to be avoided through meditation."[14] We are not condemned to eternally generate the same painful wave patterns again and again forever repeating actions based in ignorance. The purpose of Yoga is the cessation of pain through mastering and controlling the wave-generating complex, the mind and the actions which it engenders. This technique takes many forms, depending upon the proclivities of the practitioner, and the wide range of methods cited indicates that Yoga may be applied in a variety of situations.[15]

According to the commentator Vyāsa, two primary forms of yoga are outlined by Patañjali. One, described in the first section of the text *(Samādhi Pāda)*, is for the "Yogin with an engrossed mind." The other, described in the second section *(Sādhana Pāda)*, is for the "devotee with a distracted mind." Actually, the latter may be regarded as a preliminary stage; once the mind has been brought under control, one takes up the practices prescribed in the first section. But let us begin with a brief analysis of the forms of practice required if one is not as yet prepared for the more subtle stages. These techniques are outlined in the second section *(Sādhana Pāda)* in eight stages or limbs *(aṅga)*. Within these eight, the manifested world is dealt with aspect by aspect in a manner that approximates the reversal of the Sāṃkhyan process of world creation. All actions, all thoughts are brought into scrutiny and subjected to a purificatory process. One's actions and interactions in the world are first brought under control through the application of ethical abstinences and observances. The abstinences *(yama)* involve holding back from actions that build negative impressions. They are the practice of nonviolence *(ahiṃsā)*, truthfulness *(satya)*, non-theft *(asteya)*, sexual purity *(brahmācarya)*, and non-possession *(aparigraha)*. The second phase *(niyama)* requires the observance of particular activities that are conducive to the quest for liberation. These include purity *(śauca)*, contentment *(saṃtoṣa)*, austerity *(tapas)*, study *(svādhyāya)*, and devotion to the one who remains forever uninvolved with *prakṛti (īśvara-praṇidhāna)*. Through these regulatory activities, applied in day-to-day life, one minimizes the distractions that arise due to intercourse with the world. Once this has been accomplished, one focuses directly on the body through the perfection of yoga postures *(āsana)* and control of the breath *(prāṇāyāma)*. These activities further ground one within oneself and diminish the involvement with external activities. Only when these have been mastered can one achieve the detachment *(pratyāhāra)* stage of yoga, necessary to tackle the more subtle aspects of one's existence such as the impressions, residues, and habituations of the mind. The final three stages, often called "Inner Yoga," are concentration *(dhāraṇā)*, meditation *(dhyāna)*, and *samādhi*. *Samādhi*, which will be left untranslated, literally means "putting together," being derived from the verbal root *dhā* (put, place), prefixed with *sam* (together) and *ā* (unto). It is a unitive state of awareness in which the coincidence of subject, object, and means of perception is achieved. This state involves the cessation of mental modifications and, hence, may be referred to as a state of liberation. Each of these practices, from the cultivation of nonviolence to proficiency in *samādhi*, serves to lessen the influence of the afflictions on action and thereby cuts away at the root that binds one to the unending cycle of action, habit, and repeated action.

For the one mentioned earlier whose mind is engrossed, the practice of *samādhi* is all that is required for the experience of liberation. The first section of the *Yoga Sūtra*, the *Samādhi Pāda*, lists several stages of *samādhi*, beginning with concentration on gross objects that progressively becomes more subtle. The first four are referred to as *samādhi* with object *(saṃprajñatā)*. The initial stage is *savitarka*, wherein one focuses on a manifest object using words and their meaning to keep the mind steady. This gives way to a merging of the mind with the object without the interference of any thoughts or judgments, designated as the state of *nirvitarka*. Next, one's attention is turned to that which has no outward manifestation. These objects of concentration, according to the modern commentator Hariharānanda Araṇya, can include the subtle elements from which the gross world emerges (see the section on Sāṃkhya in the last chapter), the sense-of-self, the intellect, and/or *prakṛti.*[16] In the beginning of this meditative practice, called *savicāra,* one uses mental imagery to "build" concentration. Then, in *nirvicāra,* one enters into a state of oneness with the subtle object wherein the use of thinking is no longer required.

When the higher forms of concentration are achieved, the world of manifestation is called back to its source: *prakṛti* is held in abeyance and the practitioner is ready for the vision that discerns between the world of change and one's true consciousness or self. The practice of *samādhi* is summarized in the following *sūtra:*

> [The accomplished one] of diminished
> modifications, like a precious (or clear)
> jewel assuming the color of any near object,
> has unity among the grasper, the grasping, and grasped.[17]

Neither subject nor object, perceiver nor world, can be seen as substantial or separate. There is no longer any patina of interpretation applied to the object or condition at hand: it shines *(nirbhāsa)* as if it were empty of inherent form *(svarūpa-śūnya).*[18] At an even higher level, knowing and knower "lose" their independent status as well: the analogy of radiance or clarity extends to oneself *(adhyātma).*[19] Finally, all distinctions of grasper, grasping, and grasped dissolve. Total transformation has taken place, in which there is not even the slightest tendency to separate a self from things or vice versa.

These states of *samādhi* are said by Patañjali to obstruct the effects of the residue of past action *(saṃskāra).*[20] The yogin is operating on the most subtle of levels and radically reordering the tendency to continue generating and being captivated by the manifest realm as it has habitually been brought forth. Ultimately, the state of seedless *(nirbīja)* or object-less *(asaṃprajñatā) samādhi* is achieved, which burns out all afflicted influences from the past and brings about the total suppression of the mind's fluctuations. For such a person, the highest state of solitude *(kaivalyam)* has been achieved. In the last section of the *Yoga Sūtra,* this final state is referred to as *dharma-megha samādhi,* which literally translates as "cloud of virtue concentration."[21] One is said to be "disinterested even in omniscience" and a perpetual state of discriminative discernment follows, through which one always is aware of the fundamental distinction between the world of change and pure consciousness.

Sūtra IV:30, referring to *dharma-megha samādhi*, states "from that, afflicted action ceases." Hence, the binding influence of impure past action is overcome; what remains is a "cloud of virtue." The culmination of the yoga system is found when action is cleansed of affliction and hence the practitioner no longer is deluded with regard to his or her true identity. At this phase, the true self *(ātman)* is discerned and one is disconnected from the patterns of compulsive action. The karma of such an adept is said to be neither white nor black, nor mixed; the stainless luminosity of pure consciousness is revealed as one's fundamental nature.

Recalling Patañjali's opening definition, yoga is the suppression of activities in the mind *(yogaś citta-vṛtti-nirodhaḥ)*. However, this should not be misconstrued as a negation of life; Yoga affirms the existence of the world as *prakṛti*, arguing that many people see it; therefore, it does not proceed from the mind alone.[22] The purpose of Yoga is for the practitioner to have direct access to the world without the interference of impure residues, to learn how to sever past impressions, present from a time without beginning, which obscure direct perception. The pacification of the mind helps overcome the compulsive tendency to reify the world. Only then can the ever-present, undefiled witness be revealed.

The transformation into the enlightened state requires a radical restructuring of notions of self. In conventional, subject-object consciousness *(citta-vṛtti)*, the "I" *(ahaṃkāra)* thinks it is the seer, the true self. When it is revealed that the "I" is not the seer,[23] an understanding that the seer is distinct from the seen arises, sometimes translated as discriminative discernment *(viveka khyāti)*. The *ahaṃkāra* is seen as merely a function within *prakṛti*, stimulated by the affliction of I-am-ness *(asmitā-kleśa)*. In *samādhi* the "I" no longer appropriates experience; there is a unity, a non-separation of seer, seeing, and seen. In the thirteenth chapter of the *Bhagavad Gītā,* Krishna advises Arjuna that "He who sees his self not to be the doer, he sees indeed."[24] Such a person discerns the field *(prakṛti, citta-vṛtti, ahaṃkāra)* as distinct from the knower of the field *(puruṣa)*. With this movement, the sediment of prior conditioning is cleared away and awareness becomes both subject-free *(anahamvādi)* and object-free *(nirvastuka)*. Yoga may thus be seen not as a union of a discrete self with the objective world — it is not a metaphysical mergence with nature or an abstract higher plane — nor is it a Cartesian separation of the thinker from the thing. Rather, the suppression of mental activity advocated by the *Yoga Sūtra* results in the non-separation of knower, knowing, and known and allows for a mode of action indicated in the description of *dharma-megha samādhi* that is utterly unhindered by affliction.

One of the fundamental insights of the Upaniṣads, Sāṃkhya, and Yoga is that action is preceded by thought. If one's thoughts are pure, then one's actions are pure. Yoga is the means by which the purification of thought is accomplished. We have only touched on some of the techniques in the yoga system that have been developed and practiced in order to overcome the inhibiting influences of prior action. The *Yoga Sūtra* emphasizes that the manifested world, although undeniably real, relies utterly on the activities of the mind *(citta-vṛtti)*. Two important texts, presumably postdating the Classical Yoga tradition, use a formula of "mind-only" *(citta-mātra)* to assert that mental transformation is the key to liberation. These two works, the *Laṅkāvatāra Sūtra* and the *Yogavāsiṣṭha,* are of a distinctly different literary genre. Whereas the *Yoga Sūtra* is no more than an outline given in 195 sparse statements designed to be committed to memory, the *Laṅkāvatāra* and the *Yogavāsiṣṭha* are full-blown poetic discourses, making up in elegance and poignancy of delivery what is absent in terms of technical detail. Building on the basic yogic conception of the primacy of mind, they assert that liberation is possible only by purification of the mind through meditation.

The Buddhist Teaching of Mind-Only in the *Laṅkāvatāra Sūtra*

The practice of yoga was not limited to the Hindu tradition. The Buddha emphasized the importance of meditation *(dhyāna)* in the quest for *nirvāṇa* and later Buddhist schools developed extensive treatises on the mind and its control, beginning with the Abhidharma and continuing through the tantric movements. One such school, the Yogācāra or Practitioner of Yoga tradition, includes descriptions of the mind and meditation that parallel those of Sāṃkhya and Yoga.

The *Laṅkāvatāra Sūtra*, one of the early texts of Mahāyāna Buddhism and a seminal work of the Yogācāra school, contains several references to a philosophy of mind-only, using the term *citta-mātra*. The mind is seen to play an active role in the appearance of the world, which is said to arise due to latent habits *(vāsanā)*. As long as these latencies are present and as long as the mind keeps functioning under the dictates of attachment, *saṃsāra* continues. It is only when the compulsive mind is pacified that the goal of meditation can be achieved, as seen in the following verses:

> As long as the mind is set in motion,
> it is not established in the paths (to Buddhahood).
> But when there is a turning back of the mind,
> there are neither paths nor wayfarers.[25]
>
> When there is no discernment that appearance
> is mind, then dualistic thinking arises.
> When it is discerned that appearance is mind,
> the churning of thoughts ceases.[26]
>
> With release from conceptions and
> abandonment of self-attribution,
> then there no longer exists a body;
> to me there are no objects of sense.[27]
>
> There are no Buddhas, no truths,
> no fruition, no causal agents,
> no error, no enlightenment,
> no passing away, no birth.[28]

By realizing that the process of world creation comes with the arising of mind, the grip of the world is weakened and compulsive thinking can be attenuated. Ultimately, all things are seen as essentially non-substantial, including such accouterments of religious practice as Buddhas, truths, and enlightenment itself.

The *Laṅkāvatāra* takes the mind-only teaching even one step further, making the realization of mind-only synonymous with enlightenment. The "true" nature of mind is the womb of the such-gone *(tathāgatagarbha)*, the state of Buddhahood. When the mind becomes pure, it is transformed into the Buddha's mind, as indicated in the following verses:

> When constructed phenomena are seen
> as free from inherent existence or cause,
> this decidedly is mind-only,
> indeed, I call this mind-only.[29]
>
> All this is mind-only.
> The two-fold mind generates
> the existence of perceiver and perceived.
> But self and that which belong to it are never known.[30]
>
> Mind is all; it is found
> everywhere and in every body.
> Multiplicity is grasped only by those who are impure.
> Indeed, in mind-only there are no marks *(lakṣana)*.[31]
>
> When the mind-faculty ceases,
> disturbances of the mind are abandoned.
> By understanding all things *(dharma)*
> the mind becomes Buddha, I say.[32]
>
> Suchness, emptiness, excellence,
> *nirvāṇa*, realm of truth,
> the various bodies made from mind—
> I call these Buddha.[33]

Through the realization of mind-only, consciousness itself has been purified and now reflects the purity of the Buddha himself.

The *Laṅkāvatāra* holds the position that all "things" in the conventional sense do not have an inherent reality but depend on the workings of the mind. The functioning of the mind at a mundane level creates and reinforces attachment. The understanding of that process, which involves the creative power of thought, is the first step towards liberation. By recognizing that reality can only be ascribed to the grasping mind and not to things-in-themselves, the power of grasping is lessened. Once the world is considered to rely on one's perceptions of it, the bank of past impressions or residue *(saṃskāra)* and habit patterns *(vāsanā)* is purified. These impressions include even notions of enlightenment; conceptualization of any absolute must also fall away.

In summary, it is posited in the *Laṅkāvatāra* that all "things" proceed from the workings of the mind, which in turn is seen as phantasmagorial. First, the world is regarded to be like an illusion; then the mind itself is overturned; eventually all conceptualization of even an absolute falls away, revealing a state not unlike the seedless *samādhi* of the *Yoga Sūtra*. In this final state, Buddhahood is attained.

Mind-Only in Later Hinduism: The *Yogavāsiṣṭha*

The Yogācāra school of Buddhism, which promulgated the mind-only theory, has been regarded by some Buddhist scholars as imitating Hindu doctrine.[34] In turn, this form of Buddhism influenced thinkers of the Hindu Renaissance, which began in the seventh and eighth centuries C.E. One text in particular, the *Yogavāsiṣṭha*, extensively uses the mind-only formula in its explanations of the world appearance.[35] Several parallels exist between the *Laṅkāvatāra* and the *Yogavāsiṣṭha*. Both texts describe mind *(manas)* as a creative force. Both negate the independent reality of the world, claiming that all appearances depend upon the mind. Both assert that through the purification of past impressions enlightenment can be achieved. Both emphasize meditation as the means to this end. Although the Buddhist teaching of mind-only gave rise to a formalized school of thought, the Hindu use of this doctrine has been limited primarily to the Upaniṣads cited above, the *Yogavāsiṣṭha*, and the Emergence through Perception School *(dṛṣṭi-sṛṣṭi)* developed by Prakāśānanda, a Vedāntin of the sixteenth century who referred often to the *Yogavāsiṣṭha*.

In the *Yogavāsiṣṭha* discussions of mind-only,[36] the intrinsic reality of the external world is brought into question and dismissed as a type of illusion, a phantom of our imagination:

> Whatever appears in the mind
> is like a city in the clouds.
> The emergence of this world is no more
> than thoughts manifesting themselves.[37]
>
> Like the appearance of water in a mirage
> or the sight of two moons in the sky,
> so from perception do existent things appear
> although they do not exist in reality.[38]

The world emerges only upon perception. No thing or event can be positively reified or separated from perceptive processes. However, although the text is quick to dismiss notions of abiding reality, it does not allow for the extreme view of total negation. The following verse, in a dialectic similar to that used by the Mādhyamika Buddhists, systematically denies both positive and negative assertions, emphasizing that liberation hinges on the nature of the mind, not on speculation about reality or non-reality:

> Existence and non-existence and
> the perception of dissolution and creation
> are manifestations of thought;
> such things are neither true nor untrue,
> but are extensions of the mind.[39]

Poetic examples are given that extol the power of mind:

> As leaves, flowers, and fruit
> are seen to be latent in the sprout,
> so everything that is seen
> whether one is awake or dreaming
> is of the mind.
>
> As a golden image is none other than gold,
> so the activities undertaken when waking or sleeping
> are none other than thought.
>
> As foam, drops, and shower
> are all forms of water,
> so all the wonderful perceivable things
> are formations of the mind.[40]

The analogy of the sprout implies that all experience lies waiting to emerge when conditions ripen, similar to the seeds lying dormant in the storehouse consciousness *(ālaya-vijñāna)* of Yogācāra and the past impressions or residue *(saṃskāra)* in Yoga. The image of all golden objects sharing the same essence is a standard Vedāntic illustration used to describe the all-pervasiveness of Brahman. The identity of water with its various forms is a Buddhist metaphor for the non-substantiality of all constructed phenomena. Thus, these verses skillfully draw upon imagery from numerous traditions to support the point that all things arise due to the mind.

The preceding examples, although asserting that without mind no world can be known, do not describe the mind as taking an assertive role in determining how the world is perceived. In the following verses, a creative, constructive power is attributed to mind:

> Whatever thought is held with certainty,
> that very thing comes into existence
> just as a fire-ball ignites
> from contact with fire.[41]
> The mind, indeed, is the maker of the world.
> The mind, indeed, is called the person *(puruṣa)*.
> What the mind resolves to do
> comes to be through exertion.[42]

The implication that mind is to be identified with *puruṣa* echoes statements in the *Laṅkāvatāra Sūtra* that when the power of mind is known one's highest nature is revealed.

Another portion of the *Yogavāsiṣṭha* uses the term *manas* to describe a functioning of mind that corresponds to *buddhi* in the Sāṃkhya system. *Manas* is said to be the go-between that allows for manifestation; the world is said not to arise from consciousness *(cetanā*, a synonym for *puruṣa)* nor from the unconscious *(jaḍa*, which means stupid or dull, synonymous with *prakṛti)*. It is only the mind that can activate the world-creating process that allows for existence:

> The world arises from neither the conscious
> nor the unconscious.

> The mind is the cause of all things,
> Just as light reveals their forms.[43]

As in the *Sāṃkhya Kārikā*, where the world cannot emerge until intellect arises out of *prakṛti*, so in the above example the objective realm cannot be known without the mind. In Sāṃkhya the intellect serves as the link between the unconscious *prakṛti* and the silent, witnessing *puruṣa;* in the *Yogavāsiṣṭha* all experience and the world itself relies on the power of the mind.

The mind joins together two otherwise unreconcilable realms. Without mind no experience would be possible. All factors of the knowledge process — knower, knowing, and known — are said to involve mind:

> The notions of agent, action, and result;
> seer, sight, seen, and so forth,
> are all only thought.[44]

Subjectivity, activity, and objectivity all utterly depend on thought processes. The doer cannot be separated from the deed or doing, and all takes place through the facility of the mind.

The realization of the mind's power is said to bring great peace, as well as liberation. The sage Vasiṣṭha, the principal teacher in the *Yogavāsiṣṭha*, tells his royal student Rāma:

> Having heard that all this
> is no more than thought, Rāma,
> your questions will be resolved
> and you will renounce the influence of past actions.
> These three worlds and all of creation
> are no more than modifications of mind.
> When you understand this, you will achieve
> great peace within yourself.[45]

The world-creating process, when set in motion by a deluded and impure mind, results in suffering. Once the mind has been purified and understands its own power, the influences of past compulsive action are worn away. When the "play of thought" is revealed, the tendency to perpetuate world-engendering thoughts and their attendant actions ceases. As in the *Sāṃkhya Kārikā* where *prakṛti,* once revealed, hides from view, the world is said to disappear:

> The deluded mind is the agent
> who activates the establishment of creation.
> The impure mind spins out this manifold world.[46]
>
> Once established in the view that
> the form of creation is only mind emerging,
> then the physical body and so forth are not seen,
> like oil disappearing in sand.[47]

The first step to liberation is when the mind desires its own pacification. Then, when all desires are stilled, the goal has been attained:

> The mind, through consideration
> in the mind, desires dissolution.
> It is only by dissolution of the mind
> that the most excellent comes to be.[48]
>
> When there is liberation from all conceptualization,
> then the living being is in the stainless Brahman,
> as when blueness pervades the clear sky.[49]

When the world-creating conceptualizations of the mind cease, the state of liberation is attained. Through the purification of past influences, the mind no longer grasps for objects and reaches the "most excellent," wherein all differentiations dissolve.

In the various approaches to mind that we have investigated in the Upaniṣads, the *Sāṃkhya Kārikā,* the *Yoga Sūtra,* the *Laṅkāvatāra Sūtra,* and the *Yogavāsiṣṭha* a common theme is indicated: that the mind is of great importance for determining how the world is experienced. Furthermore, the emphasis on mind affirms the need for meditation, with its culmination in the dissolution of conventional, limited consciousness in favor of entry into a higher state of unitive attention, described as the true self in the Upaniṣads, isolation *(kaivalyam)* of *puruṣa* from *prakṛti* in Sāṃkhya, *samādhi* in Yoga, the uncovering of Buddha-nature in

Yogācāra Buddhism, and the attainment of liberation *(mokṣa)* in the *Yogavāsiṣṭha* (to be discussed in more detail in the next chapter). However, the simple formulaic statement "mind-only" has resulted in a debate among scholars as to its authentic intent. At one extreme Chatterjee asserts that the doctrine in Yogācāra texts represents a full-blown idealism in the sense of the Western philosophical idealist tradition. He writes that:

> Yogācāra declines the notion of objectivity, but the subjective becomes ontological: it really exists, while the objective does not.[50]

On the other hand, Willis hesitates to regard mind-only as a philosophical concept:

> *Citta-mātra*, throughout the early Yogācāra, should be more properly rendered as "just thought" or "merely thought" and seen more appropriately as functioning within the realm of discourse concerned with meditative experience — that is, within discourse about spiritual *practice* as opposed to strictly philosophical theory.[51]

It is clear that Chatterjee has missed the point: Buddhism never affirms the absolute nature of a subjective self.[52] The "mind-only" doctrine operates to undermine fixed notions of reality, including both objectivity and subjectivity. It stands as an aspect of practice, not only as a philosophical position.

The analysis of mind in the texts cited above serves to underscore the need for meditation and self-purification.[53] Whether in its Hindu or Buddhist formulation, the mind-only teaching affirms the existence of a great power within the workings of the mind which hence affects one's actions in the world. The very act of meditation, in both the *Yogavāsiṣṭha* and the *Laṅkāvatāra Sūtra*, involves the tremendous task of altering and ultimately dissolving both the world and the workings of the mind through the transformation of mind. As we will see in the next chapter, this special ability is illustrated in the *Mahābhārata* with stories and is praised in discourse; in the *Yogavāsiṣṭha,* this world-altering power is thematized in a doctrine of creativity *(pauruṣa).*

4

Effort in the *Mahābhārata* and the *Yogavāsiṣṭha*

We have seen how various textual traditions negate the reality of a self-existing world free from dependence on the senses and the mind. In the *Ṛg Veda,* sacrifice is the basis for the emergence and responsible maintenance of the world. The Upaniṣads emphasize the importance of the senses in the apprehension of the world and extol the power of mind as a constructive force. In Yoga and Sāṃkhya, techniques are outlined for mastery of mental modifications. And in the *Laṅkāvatāra Sūtra* and *Yogavāsiṣṭha* the philosophy of mind-only similarly regards thought as the key to attachment or liberation. In fact, for each of these systems, the mind is the pivot, swinging either to ignorance or to liberative knowledge. Through the creative power of mind, the world of action is constructed; through pacification of mind, the fixed reality of things melts. What determines in which direction thoughts will sway? Is the unfoldment of life as bondage or liberation left solely to one's past history, or to the gods, or does each person have control over his or her destiny? Or is life essentially unpredictable, left to chance, with forgotten actions returning to haunt us at any moment? The answers to these questions are best found in Indian literature in the form of stories that relate the experiences of persons directly involved with the drama of human life, with actively countering death and despair with positive expressions of life. For these stories we need to turn away from the texts that formed the mainstream of Indian sacrificial and philosophical tradition to a somewhat more lively and diverse genre of literature: the epics and the purāṇas.

Among the warriors *(kṣatriyas)* and rulers, a group of bards *(sūtas)* told stories of epic conquest and narrated dialogues between nobles and their advisors. These stories captured the imagination of the people and continue to be told, primarily in the tales of the *Mahābhārata*, the *Rāmāyaṇa*, and numerous other adventure texts of more recent origin referred to as the purāṇas. Although epic and purāṇic literature primarily emphasizes the acts of kings and deities, it has also been used as a vehicle for communicating philosophical traditions.[1] For instance, the *Mahābhārata* is peppered with discourses such as the *Bhagavad Gītā* and some of the eighteen books that compose the epic have explicitly philosophical designators, such as the Teaching Book *(Anuśāsanaparvan)* and the Liberation Book *(Mokṣaparvan)*. The *Gītā* is noted for its synthesis of the Brahmanical concern for maintaining the ancient rites with the active warrior ethic in the concept of *dharma*, which will be discussed in more detail in the last chapter.

The Story of Sāvitrī and Satvayat in the *Mahābhārata*

While the texts we have hitherto examined have presented a glowing if somewhat technical portrayal of the power of the mind, Kṣatriya stories provide graphic and sometimes fantastic illustrations of the efficacy of mental strength. One such story is told in the third book of the *Mahābhārata*, the Book of the Forest *(Āraṇyakaparvan)*. Yudhiṣṭhira, the head of the Pāṇḍavas and older brother of Arjuna, asks his teacher Mārkaṇḍeya if there has ever been a woman as great as Draupadī, who took all five Pāṇḍava brothers as husbands.[2] Mārkaṇḍeya replies that indeed a woman rivaled Draupadī in her devotedness, and her name was Sāvitrī. Sāvitrī was born to the King Aśvapati after he had performed great *tapas* in honor of the goddess Sāvitrī in hopes that she would reverse his accursed childlessness. His wish having been fulfilled, he named his daughter after the goddess. She grew up to be a beautiful maiden, but did not readily attract a husband, as her great splendor kept potential suitors away. Desirous that his daughter marry and bear heirs, King Aśvapati granted Sāvitrī permission to seek out her own husband. After many adventures, she chose Satyavat, a Salva prince whose father, King Dyumatsena, had been dethroned because of blindness. King Aśvapati's advisor Nārada, having reviewed the marriage candidate, decided that he indeed was worthy, being splendid, wise, handsome, noble, and friendly. However, the seer foresaw one major flaw, a great impediment to the wedding which Sāvitrī so fervently desired. In one year's time, Satyavat's life would expire, leaving Sāvitrī a helpless widow. Despite the many protests of her father and his advisor, Sāvitrī could not be dissuaded from her choice and soon married Satyavat.

The newlyweds joined Satyavat's family, which had been banished to a forest retreat due to King Dyumatsena's handicap. Unfortunately, the young bride Sāvitrī could not be happy, as she continually thought of her beloved husband's imminent demise. Months passed until finally, four days before the appointed date of death, Sāvitrī took on a vow of extreme *tapas* and stood in one place, not moving for three days and three nights. In honor of her steadfastness, Satyavat's family and the holy men at the retreat gave her special blessings.

A few hours after she had completed her sacrifice, Satyavat decided to go into the forest to gather fruit and Sāvitrī was, of course, quick to follow. After working for some time at picking fruit and splitting wood, the prince became weary and lay down on the ground, his head on his wife's lap. Suddenly, the red-eyed Yama, the God of Death, appeared with his noose and snatched from the chest of Satyavat a person in the likeness of the prince but merely the size of a thumb. Satyavat's body stopped breathing and began to stiffen. Yama set off with his catch and then turned, advising Sāvitrī to arrange her husband's funeral. But the devoted wife refused to be left behind and, by the power accumulated by her *tapas* the three days and three nights before, ran in fast pursuit of Yama. After she made her plea, Yama, impressed with Sāvitrī's devotion to her elders and husband, granted her a boon, with the stipulation that it could not include the release of her beloved. Without hesitation, she asked that her father-in-law's sight be restored. This was granted and Yama set off again, holding the thumb-sized Satyavat tightly in the noose. Undaunted, Sāvitrī persisted in following. Surprised by her perseverance, the God of Death granted three more boons, again stipulating that they not include a request for the return of Satyavat's life. She then asked that Dyumatsena be reinstated as king, that her own father be blessed with more offspring, and that she herself give birth to children. These were granted. Yama again departed, but Sāvitrī, in a show of strength, convinced him to stop and made the following impassioned speech:

> The strict always abide by the Law,
> The strict do not tremble, nor do they despair.
> The meeting of strict with strict bears fruit,
> From the strict the strict expect no danger.
> With their truth do the strict give lead to the sun,
> With their penance the strict uphold the earth.
> The strict are the course of future and past,
> They do not collapse in the midst of the strict.[3]

Awed with her fine elocution, Yama granted her one final wish, omitting any conditions. Sāvitrī seized the opportunity and successfully procured the release of her husband. Husband and wife were reunited; King Dyumatsena regained his eyesight and his reign; Sāvitrī's father and mother produced more offspring; and Sāvitrī herself "over a long period of time gave birth to a hundred gallant and never-retreating sons, who increased her fame."[4]

Through strict adherence to her vow to save her husband, Sāvitrī was able to reverse the course of fate. Despite the fantastic hyperbole, the story underlines a distinctly Kṣatriya philosophy based on human voluntarism. *Tapas* is used not strictly for the purposes of transcendence but also to secure happiness within human life, generating a power that transforms the course of *karma* and brings about new worlds of being for Sāvitrī and her family.

Effort in the *Mahābhārata*, XIII:6

In the thirteenth book of the *Mahābhārata*, the Teaching Book *(Anuśāsanaparvan)*, an Upaniṣad-style dialogue takes place on the topic of human effort *(puruṣa-kạra)*. The chapter opens when Yudhiṣṭhira asks Granduncle Bhīṣma "Is the course of a person's life already cast, or can human effort shape one's life?" In response, Bhīṣma, an ascetic renowned for his great wisdom, tells of a conversation held between Brahmā, the Lord of Creation, and the sage Vasiṣṭha. Vasiṣṭha is an ancient figure to whom is attributed the seventh book *(maṇḍala)* of the *Ṛg Veda*. Said to have been born from a pot,[5] Vasiṣṭha is especially recognized for his hymns invoking Varuṇa, the god of goodness and order. Two sons of Vasiṣṭha are mentioned in the *Ṛg Veda*, and it has been speculated that he originated a lineage of revered counselors. At a later phase of Indian literature, Manu refers to Vasiṣṭha as one of the primal sages, and the Vasiṣṭha name appears in the title of a prominent work on Hindu social ethics, the *Vasiṣṭhadharmaśāstra*.[6] Śaṅkarācārya, in his commentary on the *Bhagavad Gītā*, refers to Vasiṣṭha as the first sage of the Vedānta school.

Vasiṣṭha's views on *karma* as he learned them from Brahmā are clearly stated in this chapter of the *Mahābhārata*, though they are by no means to be regarded as the only interpretation within Hindu thought; the Indian tradition contains numerous perspectives on this issue, including the position that time is responsible for the course of action, or that the gods are truly in control.[7]

From the onset, however, Brahmā emphatically states that what may seem to be attributable to an unexplained fate in fact arises because of a preexisting seed. The nature of the fruit, which is the circumstance in which one finds oneself, depends on the quality of past action. Hence, what due to ignorance may be considered the product of the gods or fate *(daiva)* is in fact the result of human effort *(puruṣa-kāra)*:

> Nothing is born without seed;
> without seed there can be no fruit.
> From seed arises seed.
> It is known that fruit comes only from seed.
> Just as a farmer plants
> a certain type of seed
> and gets a certain crop,
> so it is with good and bad deeds.
> Just as a field sown without seed is barren,
> so without human effort there is no fate.[8]

Brahmā claims that through activity in the world, a seed is formed, made from human effort. This seed becomes one's fate and ripens when the proper circumstances arise:

> The field is seen to be the effort of a person,
> while fate is the seed.
> From the union of field and seed
> a crop flourishes.[9]

The result of past action is seen to fructify in the future. The question of fate in Vasiṣṭha's philosophy is not one of external predetermination: he mentions no controlling element, no god who dictates what form a person's life will take. It is one's actions alone that make up the code of fate; the seed produced today bears the same structure as the one that produced it. Yet, through effort and the cultivation of a particular kind of action, the seeds, the code components of future experience, can be altered. Action is the key to this change:

> The doer himself enjoys the fruit of his action.
> This is seen clearly in the world
> in regard to activity and inactivity.[10]

If one acts, a future world is cultivated. If one does not act, then the world is seemingly left to chance though in fact the future will be comprised solely of left-over, forgotten seeds of the past.

Vasiṣṭha learns two points in regard to the nature of human causation. The first message is an ethical one: if one commits an evil act, then evil will certainly follow at some undetermined point in time. The second message comes in the form of supportive statements: action is the only means to fulfillment.

> Happiness comes due to auspicious actions;
> suffering results from evil actions.
> By action, all things are obtained.
> By inaction, nothing whatsoever is enjoyed.[11]

Several didactic examples are given to reinforce the argument for ethical propriety, showing that one's actions will bring requisite punishment or reward. One heinous error is that of telling a lie:

> Vasu, although having sacrificed a hundred sacrifices
> and being like a second Vāsava,
> was condemned to the underworld
> due to one false statement.[12]

Others were doomed to equally hideous fates due to evil activities. Nṛga was transformed into a lizard, Janamajeya and Vaiśaṃpāyana were punished for unjust murders, and Saudāsa became a man-eating demon due to his infraction against a great seer.[13]

Yet, the main thrust of Brahmā's speech is not an appeal for moral action based on the generation of fear. Rather, the main concern is to demonstrate the efficacy of activity. All attainment is ascribed to action, and it is said that even gods and celestial bodies were once men who, through their efforts, reached an exulted state. At the root of all things is self-power.

> Heaven, enjoyment, and the desired state
> are all attained by actions of human effort
> here in this world.
>
> The heavenly lights, the gods, the Nāgas,
> the Yakṣas, the sun and moon, and the Māruts
> have all gone from the status of men
> to that of gods through their human effort.[14]

The self, indeed, is one's own enemy and friend,
as the self is the witness of action performed
and not performed by the self.[15]

This last verse hearkens back to the Upaniṣadic teaching that without the organization of consciousness, all actions, all effort and exertion would be meaningless.

Inactivity is condemned by Brahmā as the bane of all existence. Without activity, nothing can be accomplished. Even if one encounters an unexpected occurrence due to past action, it is not disturbing if one is firmly anchored in present action. If, however, one is not active, then one is at the mercy of the situation and unable to fend off the unexpected or to accomplish much of anything.

In all cases, a doer who is harmed by fate
does not get knocked off base,
while a non-doer gets a sprinkling of salt in his wound.[16]
It is difficult to pursue the enjoyment of
wealth, friends, power, noble birth, or success
for those who are inactive.[17]
Success does not come to those who are
stingy, impotent, or lazy,
nor to those whose conduct is neither virtuous nor valiant,
nor to those who are distressed.[18]

Inactivity is closely associated by Brahmā with reliance on fate *(daiva)*. He has explained that fate is mere fiction, a dangerous form of acquiescence to the consequences of prior action. Nonetheless, some people needlessly waste away, surrendering their life to a fate that is pure delusion.

That inactive person who follows the course of fate
without having done any human deeds
becomes weary in vain
just like a woman with an impotent husband.[19]

Human activity follows the seed of past action, which some people call fate, but this "fate" is incapable of producing anything for anyone in the absence of activity. Deeds conform to fate, but fate cannot exist without deeds.

If one's action bore no fruit,
then everything would be of no avail.

If the world from fate alone,
it would be neutralized.[20]

Hence, it is clear that action must be taken in order for the world to be created and sustained.

Brahmā extols action as the means to obtain any desired result. This power is the means to gain release from evil. Brahmans use it to make their pronouncements effective; the Kṣatriyas use it to accomplish success in war.

Having procured that which is difficult to obtain,
one casts off all sin in this world.
Fate cannot rescue a person
who has fallen into infatuation and delusion.[21]
Do the sages, disciplined by austerity and *tapas,*
and firmly holding to their vows,
send out their curses from the power of fate
and not by action?[22]
The kingdom of the Pāṇḍavas,
which had been taken by the great strength of
Dhṛtarāṣṭra's sons,
was regained not by fate,
but by the taking up of arms.[23]

Clearly, Brahmā exhorts self-action over and against all dependence on the external stimulus of fate. He asserts that through action one can cultivate a beneficial future and that one can work at minimizing the influence of the past.

As a small fire becomes large
when stirred up by the wind,
so does good fate *(sādhu-daiva)* grow
when linked with action.
As a light fades for want of oil,
so fate fades from the diminution of action.[24]

Vasiṣṭha's lesson is concluded when Brahmā again emphasizes that human effort determines the future. If one desires a new course and acts accordingly, it will be obtained. But if one relies on the past, thinking that fate is in control, no change is possible.

Fate leads one astray.
There is no power in fate. . .
Human effort, frequently practiced

with action prompted by desire
leads one to a new, unobstructed fate
in each case.

Through the rise of fate
by action already undertaken
and by action in accordance with precept
the path of heaven is obtained.[25]

In this final verse, Brahmā acknowledges that the past does contribute to the composition of the present; fate, when regarded as the product of one's past action is a factor to be reckoned with. With this knowledge, one is freed to build a world — even perhaps a path to heaven — in full cognizance that one's thoughts and actions are the creative force.

Although this story within a story, told by Bhīṣma to Yudhiṣṭhira, expresses Vasiṣṭha's philosophy of *karma* as he learned it from Brahmā, it falls short of comprising a comprehensive teaching. Several problems are left unresolved in the dialogue. It is not stated in explicit terms which forms of action are the most desirable. Also, the intention of this voluntarism is unclear. Is liberation the goal? Or is the goal found merely in the enjoyment of pleasure, the attainment of "the path to heaven"? The concept of the self is not fully defined; little or no reference is made to any relationship between what the Upaniṣads or *Gītā* might call the lower self and the higher self. Does this view of *karma* include any spiritual implications, or is this text merely a manual on how one can best perpetuate the cycle of rebirth and be successful in the search to satisfy ever-expanding desires? Although the mechanics of action are clearly expounded, the ultimate purpose of action remains obscure. As we will see in the next section, answers to all the questions posed above are resolved in a later text of Vasiṣṭha containing teachings that combine the Kṣatriya emphasis on voluntarism with the mind-only teaching and the quest for liberation.

Creativity *(Pauruṣa)* in the *Yogavāsiṣṭha*

The *Yogavāsiṣṭha,* cited earlier for its explication of

mind-only, introduces new dimensions to the discussion of *karma*. In the preceding sections, we have considered texts from various periods in the history of Indian philosophy: Vedic hymns, philosophical treatises in *kārikā* and *sūtra* form, and a few selections drawn from the *Mahābhārata* epic. These approximately span the years between 1500 B.C.E. and 300 to 400 C.E. The *Yogavāsiṣṭha* comes at a much later phase in Indian history, building on earlier traditions. It most probably went through three phases, the earliest work being a small Brahmanical, Upaniṣadic text, perhaps including the dialogue between Vasiṣṭha and Brahmā from the *Mahābhārata*. This was later expanded into the *Laghu-Yogavāsiṣṭha*, at which time the mind-only doctrine of Yogācāra Buddhism was incorporated. The third and final phase saw the emergence of a huge, encyclopedic text spanning over 29,000 verses with some sections pertaining to Śaivite Trika philosophy. This final version is said to have been composed in Kāśmir between 1150 and 1250.[26] Several commentaries have been written on the *Yogāvasiṣṭha* and several abridged versions have appeared, as well as translations into Indian languages and English.[27] Interestingly, it was considered sufficiently representative of Indian philosophy to merit no less than nine summary translations into Persian for the purpose of educating the Mughal invaders about the religions of their newly-conquered land and is said to be the first exposition of Vedānta that could be read outside India.[28] The language and style of the Sanskrit text is elegant and poetic, abounding with metaphorical descriptions, fantastic tales, and philosophical discourses that appeal to both the intellect and the imagination. Threads of Vedānta, Jainism, Yoga, Sāṃkhya, Śaiva Siddhānta, and Mahāyāna Buddhism are intricately woven into the *Yogavāsiṣṭha;* it is a Hindu text *par excellence* including, as does Hinduism, an amalgam of diverse and sometimes opposing traditions.

The *Yogavāsiṣṭha*, which might be conceived of as an addendum to the *Rāmāyaṇa*, the other of India's two great epics, consists of spiritual instruction given to Rāma by the sage Vasiṣṭha. In the opening passages, the narrator explains that after Rāma had finished his studies and had gone on many pilgrimages, he returned to his father's kingdom and was overcome with sadness. Though he had all possible human comforts and was guaranteed to rule over a magnificent country, nothing seemed to be worth the effort. He lamented that all things are impermanent, that they only come together by our imagination, that everything is like a dream, like a mirage. "All beings in this world take birth to die, and they die to be born."[29] This existential despair fills the first of the *Yogavāsiṣṭha's* six books, the "Section Dealing with Dispassion" *(Vairāgyaprakaraṇa).* Within many schools of the Indian tradition, the anguish that Rāma expresses is the first stage of the spiritual path, the perception that all is suffering *(sarvaṃ duḥkhaṃ).*[30] The second phase Rāma enters into is an overwhelming desire for release, indicated in the title of the second book, "Section on the Desire for Liberation" *(Mumukṣuprakaraṇa).* Vasiṣṭha, having become Rāma's mentor, instructs him about the need for effort in spiritual practice. This section, as we will see, contains the essential teachings of Vasiṣṭha as previously encountered in the *Mahābhārata.* The third book *(Utpattiprakaraṇa)* deals with Creation and is followed by an exposition of Existence in the fourth book *(Sthitiprakaraṇa).* These two sections explain the nature of world appearance and, through various stories, emphasize human creative power in regard to the world. The fifth book *(Upaśamaprakaraṇa)* discusses the dissolution of the world through meditation, leading to the sixth and final section *(Nirvāṇaprakaraṇa),* in which Rāma experiences the bliss of enlightenment. This last book is nearly as large as the others combined and is divided into two sections. By the end of his tutelage under Vasiṣṭha, Rāma has progressed from questioning the purpose of life, to seeking liberation, to gaining instruction from a qualified teacher as to the nature of the mind, the self, and the world. He ultimately gains proficiency in meditation and experiences *nirvāṇa.* Of particular interest in this quest for spiritual understanding is that Rāma, unlike the Buddha, returns to take up his father's kingdom, and use his newly acquired knowledge to be a better leader.

The uniquely Vasiṣṭhan thrust of the *Yogavāsiṣṭha* is found in the second book, Desire for Liberation, in which Vasiṣṭha emphasizes the concepts familiar to us from our survey of Indian literature: desire, perseverance, intention, effort, and discriminative understanding. The term most frequently used by Vasiṣṭha is *pauruṣa,* which is a strengthened *(vṛddhi)* form of the term *puruṣa. Puruṣa,* as used in Sāṃkhya, refers to the inactive witness, the consciousness that frames all experience. It is also used in the *Ṛg Veda* to designate the cosmic man who is sacrificed to create the four castes.[31] And, in the most general sense, *puruṣa* translates as man or human. The term *pauruṣa* literally means "derived from or of the nature of *puruṣa.*" In the *Sāṃkhya Kārikā,* we saw that the *puruṣa* creates nothing; all things emerge solely from *prakṛti,* who alone has the power to create. The *Yogavāsiṣṭha,* on the other hand, claims that the nonconscious arises from consciousness.[32] Hence, in this text, the *pauruṣa* seems to signify the aspect of creation closest to the purity of *puruṣa.* This would be the intellect *(buddhi)* in Sāṃkhya that, as we have seen, holds the key to liberation through its aspect of knowledge. But in the term *pauruṣa* we find a different emphasis, hinging on the derivation of the term and how Vasiṣṭha employs it. In addition to its translation of "derived from consciousness," another more literal rendering would be "manliness, the quality arising from manhood." In the case of Rāma, this might be applicable, but the other applications of *pauruṣa* belie this implied sexism. The story of Queen Chudala in the sixth book tells of a woman who holds spiritual superiority over men and uses her strength to help her mate achieve liberation.[33] And the story of Sāvitrī in the *Mahābhārata* amply demonstrates that men have no monopoly over fortitude. Hence, to convey the originary sense etymologically implied, the term *pauruṣa* will be translated as *creativity.* As context will demonstrate, the word also connotes will, strong purpose, and energy. Several other terms are used in support of the *Yogavāsiṣṭha's* voluntarist appeal, including *yatna* (effort), *prayatna* (great effort), *sāra* (resolve), *vaśa* (desire), and *samudyoga* (diligence).

In his discussion of the intellect, Īśvarakṛṣṇa outlined four dipolar aspects: virtue and non-virtue; knowledge and ignorance; non-attachment and attachment; power and impotence. In Sāṃkhya, the positive aspects *(bhāva)* are to be cultivated for obvious reasons. The *Yogavāsiṣṭha* similarly conceives of spiritual practice in dyadic terms, though the luxuriant literary style of the text and the conversational form of Vasiṣṭha's teachings make for a less systematic presentation. Nonetheless, Vasiṣṭha does speak of four linked pairs in the *Mumukṣuprakaraṇa*, each of which implies the need for strong resolution to nurture the positive aspect. The four, which are discussed in detail below, express concern for ethical behavior, purity of thought, non-reliance on the past, and creativity. Although creativity *(pauruṣa)* is included within one of the four pairs, it is needed to accomplish the positive aspects of the other three. Once these have been perfected, one gains success in life and, depending on one's desire, can achieve liberation.

Ethics

Within the Indian traditions, the taboos and mores of society are included in various texts referred to as the Dharmaśāstras. The term *śāstra* also is used for any religious or scientific treatise and, in fact, any piece of good sound advice. No specific genre of *śāstra* is cited as the supreme authority in the *Yogavāsiṣṭha*, though in many ways Vasiṣṭha's teachings are a compendium of precepts drawn from the vast *śāstra* tradition. Ultimately, the practice of ethics has to come from oneself; Vasiṣṭha denies that either teachings or teachers have the ability to convey true knowledge. However, he does assert that the words of the wise are to be followed:

> Endless bliss and equanimity
> are the highest goals of the wise one.
> He obtains them through effort.
> The virtues of the *śāstras* should be practiced.[34]
>
> Through the path prescribed by the holy men *(sādhu)*,
> calling for restraint of mind and body,
> there is creativity which yields results.
> Anything else is the struggling of an unsettled mind.[35]

The specific advice given by Vasiṣṭha is quite simple and direct. Rather than forbidding Rāma from participating in particular activities, he urges him to consider the consequences:

> In regard to the self,
> the transitory nature of the body should be considered.
> Beast-like behavior should be renounced
> and one should resort in the delight of the true self.
> Do not reduce your energy to ashes
> by indulging in the comforts
> of a house full of women
> and eating and drinking like a worm in a sore.[36]

If action is undertaken in accordance with the *śāstras* in the spirit of highest creativity *(pauruṣaparama),* then success can be achieved. It is stated that exertion in accordance with the *śāstras* allows all actions to be produced; when diligently studied, the *śāstras* lead to the highest truth.

> The highest creativity, restrained by the *śāstras,*
> is the essence of a person [literally: manliness of man].
> The desired result is held due to success.
> Otherwise, there would be no purpose.[37]
>
> Peace is not attained
> by the inactivity of ass-like men.
> Rather, it is diligence in accord with the *śāstras*
> by which success is gained in the two worlds.[38]
>
> By devotion, there (arises) the qualities of following
> the *śāstras,* etc. From the qualities of following
> the *śāstras,* etc., there is devotion.
> From mutual practice these increase, like a lotus, with time.[39]

To assist in the cultivation of an ethical point of view, Vasiṣṭha also recommends keeping good company *(satsaṅga),* making certain that one's conduct is virtuous *(sadācāra),* and heeding the teacher *(guru),* all from the time of childhood.

Purity

As in the *Laṅkāvatāra Sūtra* and the *Maitri Upaniṣad,* purification is an important aspect of self-cultivation in the

Yogavāsiṣṭha. In the ninth chapter of the *Mumukṣuprakaraṇa,* Vasiṣṭha discusses the purification of habit patterns *(vāsanā). Vāsanā,* a term used in both Patañjali's *Yoga Sūtra* and major texts of Buddhism, refers to the habits formed by impressions left in the mind and subtle body by past actions that produce an effect in the future. They are generally fraught with impurity, the afflictions *(kleśa)* of ignorance, egoism, attachment, aversion, and clinging to life. Like sediment, these dwell at the core of inauthentic selfhood and perpetuate bondage and suffering. Vasiṣṭha urges Rāma to purify himself of these habit patterns.

> Rāma, you currently possess
> habit patterns *(vāsanā)* in your mind.
> Therefore you must successfully accomplish
> the practice of purity *(śubha).*
> Although previously you did not cultivate
> this practice in regard to your habit patterns,
> if you succeed now, you will win prosperity.
> Destroy anything doubtful
> by the strong power of purity.
> If there is an increase in purified habits *(śubha-vāsanā)*
> then there can be no fault *(doṣa).*[40]

It is through *vāsanā,* generated by actions of the past, that current action takes form. Unless these are transformed, purified, and brought into accordance with *śāstra,* then one's actions in the present bear the impurities and attachments of ignorant past actions. It is only through constant purification that these old wounds can be rectified.

In language reminiscent of the Buddha's *Dhammapada,*[41] Vasiṣṭha reminds Rāma that his actions determine his future; if he acts in purity, his life will correspondingly be blessed with purity:

> By pure creativity, pure results are gained quickly.
> Impure always (follows) impure.
> That which is called fate does not exist.
>
> The one who acts with pure purpose
> meets with pure result.
> Through the impure, impurity is obtained.
> Thus, Rāma, do as you desire.[42]

The intensity of one's thought and effort determines how quickly impurity can be overcome. As we saw in the above, adherence to *śāstra* serves as the guidepost for purification:

> By as much effort as good creativity *(supauruṣa)*
> is sought, accordingly, one's impure creativity
> of the past is appeased.[43]
>
> In the case of being possessed by purity or impurity,
> the mind, from persevering effort, would prevail.
> Thus, the goal of all the *śāstras* is grasped.[44]

Non-reliance on the Past

In order to overcome impurities of the past *(prāktana)*, one must make a firm commitment to the present *(aihika)*. Vasiṣṭha points out that past actions contribute to creativity in the present, but that the past desires must be abrogated if they are impure or contrary to *śāstra*. He urges Rāma to be aware of past influences and rely solely on the present, which he declares to be stronger:

> Know that creativity is twofold,
> that of the past and that of the present.
> Through human effort *(puruṣārtha)*, the prior
> is quickly vanquished by the present.[45]
>
> Just as when two rams fight and
> the stronger prevails without much trouble,
> so there are two unequal forces of human exertion;
> that of the present overcomes the past.[46]

However, not all people have the strength to rely solely on the present and habitually fall back into old patterns. Vasiṣṭha describes such people as foolish cowards:

> He who disregards what is evident
> and relies on what is inferred (i.e., fate)
> is like the one who runs away from his own two
> hands because they look like snakes.[47]

Past mistakes are not irreversible; through resolve, the present can prevail.

> Without a doubt, the fault of the past
> is appeased by the attributes *(guṇa)* of the present.

> The aim of this is the destruction
> of yesterday's faults by today's attributes.[48]

Creativity, Success, and Liberation

The philosophy most closely associated with the sage Vasiṣṭha pertains to the efficacy of human creativity *(pauruṣa)*. As we saw in the *Mahābhārata,* this is contrasted with the notion that destiny is controlled by the gods and that men and women are ruled by fate *(daiva),* not by the consequences of their own actions. Whereas Vasiṣṭha listened to Brahmā's discourse on human effort *(puruṣakāra)* in the epic, Rāma learns the same concept in the *Yogavāsiṣṭha,* referred to as creativity *(pauruṣa)* by Vasiṣṭha.

In several verses on creativity, Vasiṣṭha asserts that reliance on fate is of no avail. Even if one attributes accomplishments to fate, they are obtained in fact by action that one has completed in the past. Reliance on fate is regarded as a handicap, stifling the possibility of liberation. Even by accepting the premise that fate exists, one is subject to the anguish of being a victim; the very thought that one is powerless leaves one impotent.

> Creativity, like the fruits of movement, is apparent.
> This is not perceived by the deluded and sluggish ones
> who infer there is fate
> (and by whom) nothing is known.[49]
>
> Whatever one strives for, that very thing
> is obtained through one's actions only.
> Yet, for the one who believes in fate,
> this is seen not to be different (from fate).[50]
>
> Having made fate non-existent here below
> by this eternally prominent thought,
> one should strive at the root of oneself
> in this existence for a better life.[51]
>
> "Fate propels me onwards!"
> Such tormented thoughts
> obscure the perception of the excellent.
> Seeing thus, prosperity departs.[52]

Vasiṣṭha proposes an argument against his own position, that the results of effort are not always quickly or readily seen, that "one does not become great through one's efforts any more than a jewel is made out of sand."[53] The response is that results must be cultivated:

> As with a perfect pot or a perfect weaving,
> restraint, steady calculation,
> and human exertion (are needed).[54]

Failure at any undertaking is due to sloth and lack of effort, not due to external forces.

> If there were not the worthlessness of sloth
> in the world, who would not be wealthy or learned?
> It is due to sloth that this ground between oceans
> is full of poor and beast-like people.[55]
>
> Those who abandon their diligence
> and take their last resort in fate
> destroy all righteousness, wealth, and pleasure
> and are their own enemy.[56]

The most basic manifestation of creativity and effort is revealed through success in day-to-day activities. Vasiṣṭha gives the following examples:

> The power of creativity is always (seen)
> through logic and by facing experience.
> It is seen bearing fruit in the world
> in someone going from one country to another.
>
> The one who eats becomes full,
> not the one who does not eat.
> The one who goes somewhere travels,
> not the one who does not move.
> The speaker is heard,
> not the one who keeps silent.[57]

It is through one's desire, whether to eat, travel, or speak, that action is performed and results are obtained. Even "involuntary" actions such as aging are seen to be due to a natural progression and not the will of the gods:

> A man is born in this world, grows up, and ages.
> There is no fate seen here,
> merely the progression from childhood to old age.[58]

In another verse, the text exposes the psychological handicap imposed by acceding to a doctrine of fate.

There is no evidence for fate
in this world nor in the other world.
By calling things fate, the fruits of action
are put into the world of heaven
(and are made inaccessible to the human order).[59]

The following three verses, taken from the seventh chapter of the *Mumukṣuprakaraṇa,* clearly summarize Vasiṣṭha's positive attitude towards creativity and effort:

Wherever there is effort of mine,
results follow quickly.
From creativity I enjoy results,
not ever from fate.

From creativity, success is seen.
The power of the wise is from creativity.
In the fragile minds of the suffering,
comfort is found only in fate.[60]

Whoever exerts himself
obtains the desired result.
For the one who stands quietly this is not so;
he obtains no results.[61]

This optimistic philosophy does not deny the possibility that man has the power to commit self-destructive acts. The *Yogavāsiṣṭha* directly addresses the problem of evil, claiming that evil arises due to one's own impure actions:

There are various reports of rich and powerful men who,
by exerting their creativity stupidly,
have become guests in hell
because of their behavior.[62]

Each person determines his or her situation by the nature of the actions in which he or she engages. If one acts in an impure manner, impurity and pain follow. If one follows the *śāstras* and relies on the present, purity is gained. Nothing is left to fate or chance.

One theme central to the *Yogavāsiṣṭha* is that one can be transformed through self-effort into a god-like condition. B.L. Atreya has termed this process "deification" and writes that "the Upaniṣads, the *Bhagavad Gītā,* and the *Yogavāsiṣṭha* all are unequivocally agreed upon Deification being the Goal of true knowledge."[63] Several gods are cited as having attained their status through effort, including Indra, Brahmā, Viṣṇu, and Śiva:

> Whoever has attained the power
> of the Noble Lord of the Three Worlds (Indra)
> has done so through creativity and effort.
>
> Anyone whose mind is illuminated,
> dwelling in the state of Brahmā,
> the Lotus-born One, has achieved
> this through creativity and effort.
>
> Any man *(pumān)* who has become a great soul,
> bearing the Eagle Banner (like Viṣṇu),
> has done so through resolve and exertion.
>
> The embodied one with the half-moon in his hair (Śiva)
> and accompanied by his wife
> has become so through creativity and effort.[64]

The implication here is that the gods symbolize powers that are accessible to the human order. Through attention paid to a particular deity, the qualities of that deity are cultivated within oneself. From the perspective of tantra, one's identity is brought into conformity with that of the chosen god *(iṣṭa-devatā)*.[65]

The final goal of creativity is not to emulate the gods. The gods are said to be restricted by their disembodied state; only humans, who are fully embodied, can achieve liberation *(mokṣa)*. How does liberation figure into the scheme of human creativity? As we have seen with the Sāṃkhya, Yoga, and Yogācāra Buddhist traditions, liberation is the antithesis of creativity, at least seemingly so. The purpose of meditation is to still the thoughts and disrupt the compulsive issuance of worlds, of *saṃsāra*. For a confirmed renouncer *(sannyāsin)* this definition of liberation conforms with the lifestyle he or she has chosen. Rāma, however, has a very specific duty to perform and eventually must return to rule his kingdom. How might he experience liberation without in fact turning his back on his responsibilities? In order to be viable, his liberation has to make sense in the context of worldly existence. Some Indic schools of thought say that liberation while living is simply not possible; the Nyāya and Vaiśeṣika Darśanas and the Vedānta philosophies of Madhva and Rāmānuja assign liberation to the realm after death. The *Yogavāsiṣṭha,* however, being in the tradition of Advaita Vedānta, Śaivism, Yoga, and Buddhism, allows for the possibility of liberation in human birth. The chapter on creativity (YV II:4) opens with an assertion that liberation is possible while in the body:

> What is the difference in the form
> of enlightenment between the embodied one
> and the one without a body?
> The two are identical,
> as is the essence of water in wave or pool.
> There is no difference at all
> in the liberation of the embodied and disembodied,
> just as the wind, whether active or calm,
> is still the wind.[66]

Although one may gain liberation, this does not negate one's humanity. Vasiṣṭha points out that a liberated person *(jīvanmukta)* appears the same as a commoner:

> Although we see before us a liberated person,
> a most excellent, solitary sage,
> he appears like an ordinary man.
> However, this does not negate his inner strength.[67]

The *Yogavāsiṣṭha* is well known for its descriptions of the liberated being, a few of which are cited as follows:

> Although externally engaged in worldly actions, he has no attachment in his mind to any object whatsoever. His conduct does not annoy anybody; he behaves like an ideal citizen and friend of all. Outwardly he is very busy, but at heart very calm and quiet. He is free from the restrictions of caste, creed, stage of life *(āśrama),* custom, and scriptures. He does not work to get anything for himself. His face is never without the lustre of cheerfulness on it. He behaves with his fellow-beings as the occasion and the status of the person demand, without the least stain on his mind. In the company of the humble, he is humble. To the knave, he appears as a knave. He plays as a child in the company of children; he is a youth among the young; he acts as an old man in the company of the aged ones. He is full of courage in the party of the courageous people and

> shares the misery of the miserable ones. There is nothing he has to achieve. He therefore performs and gives up actions without much concern, like children. In spite of his being occupied with actions appropriate to the time, place, and circumstances, he is not touched by pleasure or pain arising from them. He is full of mercy and magnanimity even when surrounded by enemies. He regards his activities as a part of the Cosmic Movement and performs them without any personal desire. He never hankers for the pleasures that are not in his hand, but enjoys all those he has. The idea of "I" and "mine," of something to be achieved and something to be avoided, has died within him. No purpose of the sage is served by any activity, nor by abstaining from activity. He, therefore, does as the occasion suits him. He is a *mahā kartā* (great worker). He works without any anxiety, egoistic feeling, pride, or impurity of heart. He is a *mahā bhoktā* (great enjoyer). He does not discard the pleasure he has got, nor desires the pleasure he had not got. He finds equal pleasure in old age, death, misery, poverty, and in ruling over an empire. He does not paralyze any one of the natural functions of his body for want of proper exercise. His body is a kingdom to him, over which he rules wisely and well. He keeps it healthy, and does not starve it of its appropriate requirements. So far as the external behavior *(vyavahāra)* is concerned, there is no difference between the liberated and the ignorant. The difference, however, consists in the presence of desire in the case of the latter, which is totally absent in the former. The life of a liberated sage is really the noblest and happiest life. From him goodness is scattered all around. Having seen him, having heard about him, having met him, and having remembered him, all creatures feel delighted.[68]

Returning to the *Mumukṣuprakaraṇa,* Vasiṣṭha makes it clear that the only way to become a sage, to achieve liberation in this lifetime, is through effort and creativity. He uses an analogy of releasing a lion from a cage:

> One is to be released by self-power *(svayam bala)*
> from this abyss of worldly existence.
> Having resorted to creativity and effort,
> one is released, just as a lion escapes from his cage.[69]

The development of liberation rests on the presupposition that consciousness and mental processes are the basis for all experience of the world. Given that the mind is the prime determining factor in one's experience, it is seen that the nature of the world relies on one's intention; the world corresponds to the thoughts that one generates. Good follows good, evil follows evil. Beyond this dualistic play of *saṃsāra* lies a third possibility: liberation, which, like any other mode of human existence, must be cultivated and nurtured. Through one's thoughts and actions, a person shapes his or her life. By means of activity executed in accordance with *śāstra* towards the goal of purifying and subjugating past influences, one can attain the highest of all possible human achievement.

The approach to life in the *Yogavāsiṣṭha* is humanistic in the most radical sense of the word, involving not only philosophical speculation, but psychological and spiritual transformation as well. According to Vasiṣṭha's teaching of creativity, the thoughts and actions of the individual must be brought into accordance with certain prescribed teachings. This is a solitary undertaking; each person must take responsibility for his or her actions. The *Yogavāsiṣṭha* asserts in several places that no teacher or teaching can bestow the experience of liberation.[70] Tools can only point to the goal and do not furnish enlightenment itself. Bondage and liberation are the result of one's own desires and Vasiṣṭha implores Rāma to develop desires conducive for *mokṣa*.

The best term to summarize the teachings of Vasiṣṭha is voluntarism, a philosophy that arises out of the perception that one's psychological attitude brings to bear a tremendous influence on how the world is perceived. It is due to the fact that one can transform the thinking process that liberation is possible. This voluntarism presupposes that in addition to consciousness of things in the world, human experience also includes a "consciousness we count on," an awareness that allows the world to be framed but which does not make itself known or manifest. This realm transcends the particular contents and activity of experience. However, without the "unseen seer," nothing could be experienced, all human activity would be arbitrary.

By the application of effort in accordance with *śāstra*, one can live in the active world as seen in the descriptions of the *jīvan mukta*. Vasiṣṭha asserts that beyond the level of cause and effect, ruled by the law of *karma*, there exists a higher truth; otherwise, there would be no purpose to exertion. But this state is not otherworldly or mystical or mysterious; it must be seen as both immanent and innate. It has been made amply clear that the *Yogavāsiṣṭha* is not concerned with heavenly realms. True knowledge is gained by purification in the present by meditation and psychological transformation. Referred to variously as *puruṣa, ātman, tathāgatagarbha,* and *śūnyatā,*[71] it is prior to the thinking process. Our world is shaped by our thoughts, but ultimate meaning is not found in our thoughts. Rather, the ultimate measure of the human condition is found in that which is beyond all forms and conception, the experience of which brings about a new way of being in the world.

The path *(mārga)* described and prescribed in the *Yogavāsiṣṭha* is in quest of that consciousness that has no object. It is a process of throwing off the binding influence of past habituations *(vāsanā)* and taking on a purified life in the present. This requires acts of creativity to restructure thought and reorder the priority given to the senses, changing the directionality and identification of one's intentions and actions. Rather than being a process of positivistic creativity, it is a creativity that dissolves the impetus of habitual world-creating patterns.

The object of philosophical inquiry in most Indic systems is realization of the true self, by whatever name. But if this true self is pure, untainted, eternal, beyond qualities, undivided, and free from predication, and the self bound in the human condition is the opposite, how can the two be reconciled? The *Yogavāsiṣṭha* offers an answer to this dilemma with its teaching of creativity, the human means by which liberation may be achieved and embodied. Without such a doctrine, the seer and the seen, *puruṣa* and *prakṛti* are forever unreconciled. Through creativity, one is free to cultivate a life of liberation.

5

Karma and Creativity

A model is presented by the relationship between Vasiṣṭha and Rāma which shows how *karma* and creativity may work in tandem in order to produce a world that is not dissonant with liberation. The model involves three aspects: wisdom, suffering, and the transition from the latter to the former. Vasiṣṭha represents the wisdom that comes through renunciation and meditation. As a revered sage, he holds the unique position of knowing the world and how it works while not being part of it. Rāma, on the other hand, has become disgusted with the suffering inherent in the world, does not understand it, and seeks release through the teachings of Vasiṣṭha. But Vasiṣṭha asserts that Rāma need not renounce all activity to obtain liberation. Rather, Rāma must fulfill his *dharma* as king. At the conclusion of the *Yogavāsiṣṭha* he is urged to rule; Vasiṣṭha points out that through his newly acquired knowledge he will be better prepared to discharge his kingly duties:

Stand in your self *(ātman)*,
in your highest, stainless existence,

liberated from all things,
performing austerity always for the sake of the self.
With your mind in the serenity of *nirvāṇa*,
beloved to the limits of your domain,
rule your kingdom with *dharma*, free from craving.[1]

Rāma's creativity in leadership will mold his kingdom; Rāma serves as the intermediary between his knowledge, which is transcendent, and his people, who are the conventional world.

Through the mode of creativity, one is allowed to continue leading an active life without the bondage of attachment. For a warrior such as Rāma, this is indispensable for the maintenance of both religious practice and the values he is required to embody and uphold as king. He combines the contemplative ideal of the Vedic and Brahmanical texts with the active role of the warrior. Furthermore, through his enlightenment, he becomes a symbol of compassion, not unlike the Buddha. His spiritual challenge lies in the administration of his kingdom: it is his responsibility to rule according to sanctified *(śāstra)* and pure *(śubha)* principles. Rāma simultaneously fulfills the roles of philosopher-king *(rājārṣi)* and regulator of the social order *(dharma-rājā)*. Having accepted and embodied the teachings given by Vasiṣṭha, it becomes his task to direct the actions within his kingdom towards those ideals. Though perhaps appearing as an "ordinary king," Rāma enacts the highest values while in embodied form, allowing the reconciliation of the phenomenal world of action with the highest dimension of human potential. As king, Rāma symbolizes the totality of existence, referred to as the Great Being *(mahāpuruṣa)* in the *Ṛg Veda*, the one who holds together the entire society.[2]

The threefold model expressed by the *Yogavāsiṣṭha* may be summarized as follows: there is pure consciousness, there is suffering, and there is a way to live with full knowledge of both. The first aspect rests on the fundamental presupposition of Indian philosophy, evident since the time of the *Ṛg Veda* and the Upaniṣads, that prior to all activity there is an unseen seer, a consciousness that allows all movement to be witnessed. In its purest form, it is called "Lord" *(Iśvara)*; in its human form it is called "*puruṣa*" or "*ātman.*" In the case of the *Yogavāsiṣṭha,* it is personified in Vasiṣṭha, who is archetypal of the Indian teacher *(guru).* The second aspect, that of suffering *(duḥkha)* is associated with the world of impermanence, the dance of *prakṛti.* Rāma's disillusionment with the world graphically describes the shortcomings of searching for meaning in the world of change. The third aspect advances the possibility that through human effort and creativity the latter world can be informed by the former: purified values can transform the world of change into an expression of higher knowledge. Vasiṣṭha himself, representing the *guru* tradition, is a perfect example. His wisdom, based on a vision of totality, is used to instruct and inspire Rāma. In turn, Rāma uses his knowledge to rule and, thus, minimizes not only his own pain but the pain of his kingdom.

This model is not unique to the *Yogavāsiṣṭha,* but reflects a pattern expressed in numerous other texts of the Hindu religious tradition, seen in dialogues between kings and sages, fathers and sons, teacher and disciples. And the message is one that has been proclaimed again and again, wherever someone seeks higher knowledge and a release from the suffering of ignorance or inability to act. The most familiar of these texts is probably the *Bhagavad Gītā,* the dialogue between Kriṣhṇa and Arjuna that, at its close, praises the benefits which accrue from listening to its philosophical explorations:

> Wherever there is Kriṣhṇa, Lord of Yoga,
> and Pārtha, the archer (Arjuna),
> there, it is my thought, will surely be
> splendor, victory, wealth, and righteousness.
> [*XVIII:78*].

Any discussion of Indian philosophical or religious traditions would not be complete without reference to the *Gītā;* therefore, in light of our journey through Hindu literature from the Vedas to the *Yogavāsiṣṭha,* we will now consider the *Bhagavad Gītā's* perspective on action and creativity.[3]

The *Bhagavad Gītā,* like the *Yogavāsiṣṭha,* arises out of crisis. Rāma's crisis was primarily philosophical in nature; Arjuna's crisis, in addition to its philosophical dimensions, is a crisis of action. Some background is necessary to convey the intricacy and gravity of his dilemma. The *Gītā* is included in the sixth book *(Bhīṣmaparvan)* of the *Mahābhārata*, and Arjuna's tale is interwoven with that of the epic. The main plot involves a dispute between cousins over rulership of the Kurukṣetra kingdom in north central India. Based on evidence from Vedic texts and geographical references within the epic, the events recounted probably took place in the eighth or ninth B.C.E., though the oldest portions of the text as we now know it probably appeared around 400 B.C.E. The text grew to its present form of approximately 100,000 verses grouped in eighteen books by the fourth or fifth century C.E.[4]

The story is reportedly told by a great seer *(ṛṣi)* named Kṛṣṇa Dvaipāyana (not to be confused with Sri Krishna), most commonly known as Vyāsa, to whom is also attributed the four Vedas and all the Purāṇas. Through a very complicated series of events, the reproductive services of this ugly holy man are needed to ensure the continuity of the ruling lineage. Vyāsa must impregnate his deceased half-brother's two wives. The first wife cannot stand the sight of him and closes her eyes through the ordeal. Consequently, her son, Dhṛtarāṣṭra, is born blind. When Vyāsa approaches the second wife, she grows pale at the sight of him. As a result, her son is born pale and therefore called Pāṇḍu, "the pale one." In due course, two groups of grandsons are born. The blind king begets 100 sons. Pāṇḍu, on the other hand, cursed for killing copulating antelopes, was warned that if he had intercourse he would die as punishment. His two wives, according to the tale, conceive five sons between them by fantastic methods. The wife Kuntī invokes the gods to impregnate her and receives three sons: Yudhiṣṭhira, by Dharma, the god of justice; Bhīma, by Vāyu, the wind god; and Arjuna, by Indra, the warrior god. Second wife Madrī cohabits with the two Aśvin gods and begets the twins Nakula and Sahadeva. These five are the Pāṇḍava brothers.

The adventures and misadventures of these two sets of cousins are too numerous to mention, but suffice it to say that they come into competition for the kingdom, which had been lost by the Pāṇḍavas to the sons of the blind king during a dice game. By prearranged agreement, the hundred sons of Dhṛtarāṣṭra are due to give back the kingdom after having ruled for several years. They refuse to abide by the contract, and the Pāṇḍavas are forced to wage war in order to regain their rightful territory. However, the cousins were raised together and shared the same teachers. The prospect of a war between the two camps is appalling, and especially repugnant because so many good friends must be killed. Thus, we arrive at the time of the *Bhagavad Gītā*, the moment just before the battle begins: Arjuna must face the anguish of killing his relatives and friends or being killed.

The *Gītā* opens with Dhṛtarāṣṭra asking his minister, Saṃjaya, to tell him what is happening on the field of the Kurus, the battlefield. Saṃjaya proceeds to list the principal warriors and then turns his attention to Arjuna and his charioteer, Sri Krishna. Arjuna asks Krishna to place the chariot in the center of the field and then sees arrayed before him his teachers, uncles, brothers, sons, grandsons, and friends. The sight overwhelms him; it is clear that all will be slain. Thinking that if all is destroyed then kingdom and pleasure would be of no use, he throws down his bow, refusing to fight, his mind overcome with grief. In the chapters that follow, Krishna takes Arjuna on a philosophical journey, bringing into question Arjuna's attachment to both himself and others. The dialogue builds until Arjuna is overwhelmed by a vision of totality, prompted by Krishna, which liberates him from his prior self-defined perspective. This experience prompts him to seek new answers from Krishna, answers that explain how to live with an understanding of life by which action becomes purposeful and liberating.

How does Krishna exact the transformation of Arjuna from a man filled with doubt to a man of great knowledge? He begins in chapter two by explaining the Yoga of Understanding *(Sāṃkhya-Yoga)*, recounting to Arjuna the insights to be gained from the Sāṃkhya philosophy. He reminds him that although contact with the objects of sense produce pleasure and pain, both are not lasting (II:14). He speaks of that which is beyond all change: weapons do not cut it; fire does not burn it; water does not wet it; winds do not dry it (II:23). He tells Arjuna that as a Kṣatriya his duty is to fight. If he loses, he gains heaven. If he wins, he gains the earth (II:37). Krishna urges Arjuna to ready himself for battle, regarding pleasure and pain, gain and loss, victory and failure as the same. Only when Arjuna has renounced interest in the fruits of his action can he find true peace.

In the third chapter, the Yoga of Action *(Karma-Yoga),* Arjuna is advised to perform the action that has to be done, staying always free from attachment (III:19). Krishna points out that it was by action alone that Janaka, the philosopher-king, attained perfection and tells Arjuna that he should act, attending to the holding together of the world *(loka-saṃgraha)* (III:20). Bringing to mind the Sāṃkhya system, he reiterates that actions are done by the *guṇas* of *prakṛti* alone; it is only the deluded one who thinks "I am the doer" (III:27). By knowing that all this is only the *guṇas* acting on *guṇas,* one is not attached. When asked by Arjuna why a man is impelled to do evil, Krishna responds that desire and anger, born of passion *(rajas),* conceal true knowledge and fuel the senses. Only by subduing the senses and controlling the mind can desire be overcome.

In a discourse on the Yoga of Knowledge in the fourth chapter *(Jñāna-Yoga),* Krishna explains that one must see action in inaction and inaction in action; only then can one be free of compulsive desire. This is accomplished by renouncing the fruit of action *(karma-phala-asaṅga)* and leads to constant satisfaction and independence. Such a one is said to do nothing, even though engaged in action (IV:20). Sacrifice is cited as the model for proper action; the sacrifice of knowledge *(jñāna-yajña)* is said to bring the completion of all action (IV:33). In the fifth chapter, the Yoga of the Renunciation of Actions *(Karma-Sannyāsa-Yoga),* Krishna further articulates the need for the relinquishment of attachment, saying that the wise ones see a cow, an elephant, a dog, an outcaste, and even a learned and wise Brahman as the same (V:18). He describes the sage intent on release as one whose senses, mind, and intelligence are controlled, who has overcome desire, fear, and anger; such a one is forever liberated (V:28). The means to achieve this are described in chapter six, the Yoga of Meditation *(Dhyāna-Yoga)*. For the one aspiring to yoga, action is the means; for the one who has reached yoga, tranquility *(śama)* is the means (VI:3). To gain yoga, Krishna advises "Giving up all desires stemming from compulsive purpose; restraining everywhere the senses with the mind; little by little, let him be stilled, with intellect *(buddhi)* firmly held and fixing the mind *(manas)* on the self *(ātman)*, he should not think of anything at all" (VI:24-25). Krishna assures Arjuna that even a small amount of practice will be beneficial.

In the next four chapters, Krishna further tells Arjuna of the highest self, and describes himself to be identical with that transcendent state. In the Yoga of Wisdom and Understanding *(Jñāna-Vijñāna-Yoga)* Krishna distinguishes between the lower *prakṛti*, which is the world of the senses and the mind, and the other, higher *prakṛti*, from which all life emerges. Both are said to have their origin in Krishna, who is the "seed of all beings." He declares that even those who sacrifice to lesser gods in hopes of receiving boons, in fact, sacrifice to Krishna, but their fruit is of little consequence. "Those who sacrifice to the gods, go to the gods; but those who are dedicated to me, go to me" (VII:23). "Only persons who are beyond the illusion of opposites and who strive for release take refuge in Krishna, and come to know Brahman, the higher self, and action itself thoroughly" (VII:29). In the Yoga of Imperishable Brahman *(Akṣara-Brahma-Yoga)*, Krishna explains *puruṣa* as the support of all things, the vision to be attained, "by whom all this is pervaded, in whom all beings stand" (VIII:22). In knowing this, all fruits of action are transcended and peace is attained. The Yoga of Royal Knowledge and Royal Mystery *(Rāja-Vidyā-Rāja-Guhya-Yoga)* contains further distinctions about the lower and higher *prakṛti* that Krishna issues forth. Those who see the higher *prakṛti* through sacrifice and devotion make their offerings to Krishna: he is witness, the final shelter; the origin, dissolution, and foundation; immortality; existence and non-existence; the enjoyer of all sacrifices. He advises Arjuna: "Make as an offering to me all your doing, eating, sacrificing, giving, and your austerities; thus you will be liberated from pure and impure fruits *(śubha-aśubha-phala)* and from the bonds of action; your self disciplined by the yoga of renunciation, you will come liberated to me" (IX:27-28). In chapter ten, the Yoga of Manifestations *(Vibhūti-Yoga)*, Krishna explains the nature of his compassion: by appearing as so many gods, from sages, trees, horses, weapons, demons, and *mantras* to purifiers, warriors, rivers, victories, Vedic hymns, and more, he has proven to be the manifestation of all that is worthy of worship, all that inspires ascension to the true self. At the end, he declares: "I support this entire universe constantly, with a single fraction of myself" (X:42).

Up until this point, Arjuna begins nearly every chapter by asking Krishna for the one path by which he may definitely reach the highest good. In chapter two, he pleads, "I ask you which would be better? Tell me for sure, I am your student; instruct me, as I have come to you" (II:7). In chapter three, he asserts, "You are confusing my understanding with these manifold statements. Therefore, tell me one thing by which without doubt I may obtain the highest good" (III:2). In chapter five, he still seeks a single answer: "Krishna, you praise the renunciation of actions and then again you praise yoga. Which one of these is better? Tell me definitely!" (V:1). In chapter six, he demands, "You must cut off completely this doubt of mine!" (VI:39). By the time of the eighth chapter he becomes slightly less frantic, asking about Brahman, the higher and lower domain, and about how sacrifice works (VIII:1-2). In chapter ten, Arjuna pointedly asks: "How may I come to know you by continuous meditation? In what form should I think of you? Tell me in more detail of your power *(yoga)* and manifestation. I am not yet satiated by the nectar of your words" (X:17-18). Finally, after so much preparation and so many discourses, Arjuna asks Krishna in chapter eleven to reveal the form that is described as Lord *(aiśvaram)* and highest self *(puruṣottama)*. He asks for a direct experience, a showing *(darśana)*: "If you think it could be seen by me, O Lord, then show to me, Prince of Yoga, your eternal self!" (XI:4). In response, Krishna reveals to Arjuna the vision that he has requested. Its description is stunning. "If there could be in the sky a thousand suns all rising at once, such splendor would be the splendor of that Great Self *(mahātman)*" (XI:12). The vision is without beginning or end; all worlds are pervaded by it. The gods stand in amazement, singing praise. Into Krishna's many mouths, studded with terrible tusks "like the devouring flames of time," are cast all the players on the battlefield: the sons of Dhṛtarāṣṭra, the sage Bhīṣma, the teacher Droṇa, and all the others. Having revealed what time will bring, Krishna tells Arjuna to stand up, to conquer his enemies. "By me they are already slain; be you merely the occasion, O Arjuna" (XI:33). Overwhelmed by Krishna's powers, Arjuna praises him as the first of gods, the primal *puruṣa,* the knower and what is to be known. After expressing homage and obeisance, he asks Krishna to return to his human form, and the dialogue once more resumes.

But now there is a difference. Arjuna has had direct experience of what has been so lavishly praised and described by Krishna. The true self is no longer a theoretical abstraction but has been revealed in embodied form. From this point onwards, in chapters twelve through eighteen, Arjuna's questions are of a different nature. He no longer implores Krishna for definite answers but asks him to further explain the nature of devotion *(bhakti-yoga)* by which he has his vision; to talk more about the difference between *puruṣa,* the knower of the field, and *prakṛti,* the field of change, both of which are aspects of the human condition. He asks more about the three *guṇas* and how they function within *prakṛti;* he finds out how the yogins see the highest self through the eye of wisdom. Krishna elucidates the distinction between liberating and binding conditions and then, finally, for the concluding chapter, explains the Yoga of Freedom by Renunciation *(Mokṣa-Saṃnyāsa-Yoga).* The contents of the chapter reflect concerns that Krishna has addressed consistently since the second chapter: sacrifice of the fruits of action, the distinctions of the *guṇas,* the cultivation of equanimity, the importance of non-doership, and so forth. The pivotal verse, which indicates that Krishna's task has been completed, is as follows: "Thus by me has this knowledge been fully expounded, which is more secret than secret. Having reflected on this fully, do as you desire!" (XVIII:63). Until this point, even after receiving the vision, Arjuna regarded Krishna as his teacher and relied on him for guidance. Krishna's statement "Do as you desire!" signals that Arjuna's knowledge has now been fully embodied, that he has reached the point where he can in full conscience act without hesitation. This is the creative moment, the moment that determines Arjuna's future world. Most importantly, the decision is his; he has taken full responsibility for his situation and for the insight that Krishna has prompted in him. Arjuna's final statement, which is most notable for his firm resolve in contrast to his lack of nerve in the first chapter, is this: "Delusion is destroyed; memory is regained by me through your grace, Unchanging One. I stand now with doubt dispelled; I will do as you have said" (XVIII:73). Having moved from helplessness to creativity, Arjuna is now free to act as he must act, not unlike Rāma, who returned to rule his kingdom.

Like the *Yogavāsiṣṭha*, the *Bhagavad Gītā* presents a model for conducting action in the world. Arjuna is confronted with a horrendous situation: having to slay his family and teachers, he pleads that inaction would be better. Krishna exhorts Arjuna to act without doership, to see that the *guṇas* in fact accomplish all things. Arjuna must shift the locus of his identity; he must see that he is not the doer. To induct him into this vision, Krishna shows Arjuna the perspectives of many yogas. It is not until chapter eleven that Arjuna is fully purged. Only when he experiences the impermanence of all things directly, do Krishna's words make sense. This revelation does not result in a state of blessedness for Arjuna, but rather allows him to relearn his sense of identity and his relationship with the world. He now is able to embody the knowledge that *prakṛti* alone changes; *puruṣa,* Arjuna's true self, remains an inactive witness. Action then is able to continue, unobstructed by Arjuna's attachment to its consequences.

This philosophy of life does not balk at the urgency of performing action. The goal is to transcend I-centered consciousness and, thus, eliminate that which separates one from circumstance. In seeing that all actions are already accomplished, Arjuna enters into a totality similar to that described in yoga wherein all distinctions of doer, doing, and act to be done dissolve. One's actions become a reflection of what is needed to uphold the world *(loka-saṃgraha)*, and one communicates this wisdom to other people through one's actions. This model is like that of the Buddha or the *bodhisattva:* once a degree of understanding has been attained, it must be used to lessen the pain of others so that they too might reach *nirvāṇa*. Madeleine Biardeau has summarized the this-worldly orientation of the *Bhagavad Gītā* as follows:

> In the teaching of the Gita, like that in the Puranic notion of *puruṣa*, liberation is tied less to an "eschaton" than to present action and this is done for the actual good of the people and not for a hypothetical liberation of all. Attention is put on the earth, on this world that the prince must make as prosperous as possible in fulfilling exactly his duties that have been assigned to him in the Brahmanic treatises.[5]

Actions are seen as interpenetrating substances, affecting more than oneself. In contrast to Farquhar's condemnation of karma, this doctrine of action is thoroughly benevolent and philanthropic.

In our discussion of *karma*, we have seen that action is inseparable from the movement of time. The three moments of past, present, and future exist in reciprocity: the present relies on the past; the present shapes the future. For those without knowledge, this is the one's predestined fate, to continually repeat the mistakes of the past, blindly moving in the unending cycle of existence *(saṃsāra)*. Release comes through knowledge, not that one is the author of action, but rather that all action is not attributable to one's true self. Only this perspective can bring liberation and allow for creativity; any other would engender the continuation of attachment to the outcome of action. Freedom is not found in forceful acts designed to create a better world, but in a recognition that past action is impenetrable; no one can predict what the future can bring, but one's attitude towards the open horizon allows one to move freely without fear of the past or the future. Although the pattern of action cannot be irrevocably erased, one's attachment can be mitigated through knowledge of the higher self.

Hinduism has given birth to two approaches to purification. One emphasizes living through life and then, in later years after one's desires have been fulfilled, calls for renouncing the world and cultivating knowledge. The other way of purification calls for detachment in action, the model proposed by Krishna in the *Bhagavad Gītā.* The first way requires that one serve as student *(brahmācārya)* in the home or *āśrama* of a teacher in order to learn not only how to support oneself, but also learn the fundamental philosophical insights of the tradition. Then one leaves, takes up life of the householder *(gṛhasta),* pursuing one's desires in the world of the senses and sense objects. After one's children's children are born and the continuity of life is assured, then and only then does one return to the quest for knowledge, becoming first a forest dweller *(vanna-prastha)* and finally a total renunciate *(saṃnyāsin).* These last two phases lie utterly outside conventional life. In contrast, the model proposed by Krishna literally brings the *āśrama* onto the battlefield, making the way of detachment in action accessible to virtually anyone. Within this system, life is affirmed without disregarding its transcendent dimension. This way of action involves creativity: working with and through *karma* as opposed to negating it. The net result of both approaches is the same: overcoming the negative influence of past action.

In some modern interpretations, the theory of *karma* seems to be riveted to a quest for personal salvation. Acts are seen to be committed by a person, accrue to that person, and must be purified by the person. The formula "If I do this good act now, I will earn a reward in the future" would be one expression of this reading, as would "the reason I am so unfortunate now is because of evil acts I committed in the past." This mechanistic view of action has spawned wonderful cults of past-life exploration, but is outside the Indian tradition in two fundamental aspects. First, it does not take into account the descriptions of one's true self as being uninvolved with *prakṛti.* Second, it ignores the fundamental message of Hinduism: that life must be upheld and that salvation is not for the good of one's biographical conceptions of oneself; in fact, it abrogates all I-centered concerns. Rather than sequential or vertical, with one act following another or leading upward to a state of blessedness, or downward to damnation, *karma* must be understood as an interpenetrating process. An action does not remain confined to one life; it cannot be restricted to the doer alone. Effects of action are widely felt. The way in which one conducts oneself is the way of culture. The world is created by action, and through one's action pain is sustained, increased, or mitigated. For Arjuna, Rāma, and the Buddha, freedom in life only became possible when they overturned all attachment to their preconceived notions of self-identity. Furthermore, their freedom consisted in a life of staggering responsibility: Arjuna had to fight through eighteen days of war and face the consequences; Rāma had to rule over a kingdom; and the Buddha devoted fifty years of his life to building a religious community *(saṃgha)* and preaching *dharma* to thousands and thousands of people. In each case, freedom is a freedom to perform action, not a freedom from performing action.

How might this model of freedom in action bear relevance for a non-Indian millieu? It helps counter two extreme views, to which a member of virtually any human society is susceptible. On the one hand, it addresses the pitfall of holding onto a strong self-image, which promotes greed in oneself and antagonism in others. On the other hand, it strengthens one's sense of dignity and self-respect, holding each person directly responsible for the creation and sustenance of his or her own world. Uniting these two dimensions results in a de-centering of self-concern for the benefit of everyone. The world becomes incorporated into being human in a literal sense: the mind, the senses, and the objects of sense compose the world and we are responsible for their construal, their use and abuse. Teachings and teachers have provided guidelines for how to live, but the responsibility lies within oneself to take up the quest for the self-understanding that in turn benefits all. How we regard what befalls us is determined by our past and will determine our future. With diligence it can be discerned that "I am not the doer"; only then can true freedom take place, a freedom for both self and others.

The social vision expressed in the various texts we have

surveyed balances the quest for a unific vision with the challenges of coping with particularized circumstances. Without experience of the former, whether called *puruṣa*, unseen seer, or *ātman*, one is bound by conventionality, bound to a fixed identity that is subject to loss and gain. Once the non-substantiality of the "lower self" is realized, the horizons become limited only by one's desires. The boundlessness found in the true self opens one to utter possibility in the conventional realm. Without the impure influences that bind a person to a fixed self-identity, multiple bodies and multiple worlds may be generated. The social implications are immense: one becomes free not to do as one is driven, but to do as is most appropriate to uphold life, to go with cultural vision, with *dharma*. Herein lies the utility of sacrifice: when one's activities are utterly purified of influence from the past, expression is truly creative, out of nothing, with a debt to nothing. Action, rather than being a fetter, becomes a joy: *karma* is creativity.

Appendix 1

A Translation of *Mahābhārata* *XIII (Anuśāsanaparvan):6**

1. Yudhiṣṭhira said:
   O Grandfather, possessing great knowledge,
   proficient in all the *śāstras*,
   tell me which is better,
   fate or human effort?
2. Bhīsma said:
   O Yudhiṣṭhira, with respect to this question
   they cite the ancient story
   of the dialogue between Vasiṣṭha and Brahmā.
3. A long time ago, Vasiṣṭha asked
   the Blessed One, Brahmā,
   which was more important:
   human action or fate?
4. Then, O king, the great lotus-born one,

venerable god of the gods,
said these sweet, significant,
and well-reasoned words:

5. Nothing is born without seed;
without seed there can be no fruit.
From seed arises seed.
It is known that fruit comes only from seed.

6. Just as a farmer plants a certain kind of seed
and gets a certain crop,
so it is with good and bad deeds.

7. Just as field sown without seed is barren,
so without human effort there is no fate.

8. The field is seen to be the effort of a person,
while fate is the seed.
From the union of field and seed
a crop flourishes.

9. The doer himself
enjoys the fruit of his action.
This is seen clearly in the world
in regard to activity and inactivity.

10. Happiness comes through pure actions;
suffering results from evil actions.
By action, all things are obtained.
By inaction, nothing whatever is enjoyed.

11. In all cases, a doer who is harmed by fate
does not get knocked off base,
while a non-doer gets
a sprinkling of salt in his wound.

12. Beauty, luck, and various riches
are obtained through austerity *(tapas)*.
All things are obtained through action.
The one who is a do-nothing obtains nothing from fate.

13. Similarly, heaven, enjoyment, and the desired state

are all attained by actions of human effort here.

14. The heavenly lights, the gods, the Nāgas,
the Yakṣas, the sun and moon, and the Māruts
have all gone from the status of man
to that of gods through their human effort.

15. It is difficult to pursue
the enjoyment of wealth, friends,
power, noble birth, and success
for those who are inactive.

16. Prosperity is obtained by the Brahman through purity,
by the Kṣatriya through valour,
by the Vaiśya through industriousness,
by the Śūdra through service.

17. Success does not come to those
who are stingy, impotent, or lazy,
nor to those whose conduct is neither virtuous nor valiant,
nor to those who are distressed.

18. Even Viṣṇu, the Blessed One,
creator of the three worlds,
the Daityas and the gods,
is enduring austerity *(tapas)* in the ocean.

19. If one's actions bore no fruit,
then everything would be of no avail.
If the world operated from fate alone,
it would be neutralized.

20. That inactive person who follows the course of fate
without having done any human deeds
becomes weary in vain
just like a woman with an impotent husband.

21. There is no fear among humans
in respect to good and evil.
Among the gods, however,
fear is generated by just a little.

22. Human activity follows fate,
yet fate is incapable of producing anything
for anyone in the absence of activity.
[Fate is constituted of past activity.]

23. When it is seen that even
status among the gods is not permanent,
how could one depend on
or promulgate fate without action?

24. The gods are not concerned
with the welfare of anyone in this world.
Out of fear of their own subjugation,
they cause formidable attachment.

25. There is always a difference
between the seers and the gods.
Why would the originators of fate
say there is no fate?
[The seers, who understand that fate
arises from action, deny there is any
such thing as fate, while the gods,
who thrive on the business of fate,
teach the doctrine of fate.]

26. How does it (action) arise,
if it comes from fate?
Even in the world of gods,
it is produced from fluctuations *(bahavaścchala).*

27. The self, indeed, is one's own enemy and friend,
as the self is the witness of action
performed and not performed by oneself.

28. Whoever accomplishes activity and improper activity
(does so) through completed action.
When action is good,
then bad deeds are not effective.

29. The gods depend on merit;
everything is obtained by meritorious deeds.

What could fate do for the man who practices merit?

30. Long ago, Yayati fell to the earth
but was again elevated to heaven
by the good actions of his grandchildren.

31. The royal sage Purūravas,
known as the descendant of Ilā,
attained heaven by the efforts of the Brahmans.

32. Saudāsa, King of Kośala, who did good actions
through the performance of the Aśvamedha
and other sacrifices
became a man-eating demon
by the curse of a great seer.

33. Aśvatthāma and Rāma,
both arms-bearers and sons of sages,
did not go to the world of heaven
except for their good deeds and actions.

34. Vasu, although having sacrificed one hundred sacrifices
and being like a second Vāsava,
was condemned to the underworld
due to one false statement.

35. Bali, son of Virocana,
bound by his righteous vow to the gods,
was consigned to hell by the will of Viṣṇu.

36. Why was not Janamejaya,
who followed the course of Śakra
having killed a Brahman woman,
restrained by his fate?

37. Why was the sage Vaiśaṃpāyana,
who out of ignorance slew a Brahman
and was tainted by killing a child,
restrained by fate?

38. Long ago, the royal sage Nṛga
was transformed into a lizard

because he had made the gift of the cow
to the Brahmans incorrectly at the great sacrifice.

39. The royal sage Dhudhumāra
became incompetent at his sacrifices and,
having forfeited the benefits,
went into a deep sleep at Gīrivraja.

40. The kingdom of the Pāṇḍavas, which had been taken
by the greath strength of Dhṛtarāṣṭra's sons,
was regained not by fate
but by the taking up of arms.

41. Do the sages, disciplined by austerity and forbearance,
and firmly adhering to their vows,
send out curses from the power of fate
and not by their action?

42. Having procured that which is difficult to obtain,
one casts off all sin in this world.
Fate cannot rescue a person
who has fallen into infatuation and delusion.

43. As a small fire becomes large
when stirred up by wind,
so does good fate grow
when joined with action.

44. As a light fades for want of oil,
so fate fades for want of action.

45. Having attained great wealth, pleasures, and women,
a man is not capable of enjoying them here without action.
These hidden treasures, protected by the gods,
approach even an impoverished man by action.

46. The world of the gods is distinguished
from the world of men:
there is much prosperity in the houses of men.
The house of the gods is seen as that of the dead.
It is not by abstention from action by people
that fate comes to fruition.

47. Fate leads one astray.
There is no power in fate.
Fate conforms to action done first as to a *guru.*
Human effort, frequently practiced by the action of desire,
leads one to a noble, unimpeded fate in each case.

48. Thus, Best of Sages,
has the fruit of human exertion,
which is always seen,
been expounded correctly by me to you.

49. Through action initiated by the power of fate,
and through action in accordance with precept,
the path of heaven is obtained.

Appendix 2

Three Chapters from the *Mumukṣuprakaraṇaṃ* of the *Yogavāsiṣṭha**

II:4 Explanation of Creativity *(Pauruṣa-vivaraṇam)*

1. Vasiṣṭha said:
   Just as the essence of water is the same
   in a rolling or calm ocean, or even in a pond,
   so is the nature of liberation the same for both
   the embodied one and the one without body.
2. Liberation, whether with or without body,
   is not found in objects.
   If food is untasted,
   how can it be experienced by the eater of food?
3. Although we see before us a liberated person,
   a most excellent, solitary sage,

he appears like an ordinary man.
However, this does not negate his inner strength.

4. What is the difference in the form
of enlightenment between the embodied one
and the one without a body?
The two are identical,
as is the essence of water in wave or pool.

5. There is no difference at all
in the liberation of the embodied and disembodied,
just as the wind, whether active or calm,
is still the wind.

6. With or without a body,
the nature of liberation does not differentiate
between "ours" and "his."
There is an undivided oneness.

7. Therefore, listen to these well-formed words,
which are like an ornament for your ear.
I am revealing to you the knowledge
which dispels the darkness of ignorance.

8. Indeed, Rāma, everything that is here
at all times in *saṃsāra*
is obtained by all
from correctly applied creativity.

9. This truth is like the rising of the moon
which inspires tranquility and delight in the heart:
the fruits of moving about *(parispanda)*
are obtained from creativity only, not from anything else.

10. Creativity, like the fruits of movement, is apparent.
This is not perceived by the deluded and sluggish ones
who infer there is fate
[and by whom] nothing is known.

11. Through the path prescribed by the holy men *(sādhu)*,
calling for restraint of mind and body,

there is creativity which yields results.
Anything else is the struggling of an unsettled mind.

12. Whoever wishes for something
and gradually strives towards that end
inevitably obtains his goal,
not the one who turns back halfway.

13. Whoever has attained the power
of the Noble Lord of the Three Worlds (Indra)
has done so through creativity and effort.

14. Anyone whose mind is illuminated,
dwelling in the state of Brahmā,
the lotus-born one, has achieved
this through creativity and effort.

15. Any man *(pumān)* who has become a great soul,
bearing the Eagle Banner (like Viṣṇu),
has done so through resolve and exertion.

16. The embodied one with the half-moon in his hair (Śiva)
and accompanied by his wife
has become so through creativity and effort.

17. Know that creativity is twofold,
that of the past and that of the present.
Through human effort *(puruṣārtha)*, the prior
is quickly vanquished by the present.

18. By efforts, by firm practices,
and with the strength of knowledge,
they are able to knock down Mount Meru.
What should one say about previous creativity?

19. The highest creativity, restrained by the *śāstras*,
is the essence of a person [literally, the manliness of man].
The desired result is held due to success.
Otherwise, there would be no purpose.

20. There are some men who, due to their desire,
have incapacitated themselves to such an extent

that they cannot squeeze their fingers together
sufficiently enough to hold water without
scattering several drops.
On the other hand, there are some who,
by efficacious actions, take on the responsibility
of seas, mountains, cities, and islands,
as well as families, for whom even the earth itself
would not be too much.

II:5 Definition of Creativity *(Pauruṣa-sthāpanaṃ)*

1. Vasiṣṭha said:
Foremost, it is active life *(pravṛtti)*,
pursued in accordance with the *śāstras*,
that is productive of all actions,
just as light produces distinctions of color.

2. Action desired by the mind
which is not in accordance with the *śāstras*
is directed to a drunken diversion.
The deluded one has no accomplishment or purpose.

3. Whatever one strives for, that very thing
is obtained through one's actions only.
Yet, for the one who believes in fate,
this is seen not to be different (from fate).

4. Two forms of creativity are known:
that in accordance with the *śāstras*
and that deviating from the *śāstras*.
Deviation from the *śāstras* produces worthlessness,
while adherence to the *śāstras* leads to the highest purpose.

5. Just as when two rams fight
and the stronger prevails without much trouble,
so there are two unequal forces of human exertion:
that of the present overcomes the past.

6. Thus, whatever is sought through human effort
will be won by a disciplined man
due to his undertaking in the present.

7. When two rams fight
or two unequal exertions are made,
the stronger of the two wins.

8. When failure occurs even when creativity
is undertaken in accordance with the *śāstras*,
then the strength of the doer of the failure
is to be ascertained by his own creativity.

9. By the application of highest creativity
to the point of gnashing one's teeth,
impurity is overcome by purity;
creativity of the past is conquered.

10. "This human effort of the past binds me."
From the direct experience
of intensifying present strength,
this thought does not recur.

11. By as much effort as good creativity *(supauruṣa)* is sought,
accordingly, one's impure creativity
of the past is appeased.

12. Without a doubt, the fault of the past
is appeased by the attributes *(guṇa)* of the present.
The aim of this is the destruction
of yesterday's faults by today's attributes.

13. Having made fate non-existent here below
by this eternally prominent thought,
one should strive at the root of oneself
in this existence for a better life.

14. Peace is not attained
by the inactivity of ass-like men.
Rather, it is diligence in accord with the *śāstras*
by which success is gained in the two worlds.

15. One is to be released by self-power
from this abyss of worldly existence.
Having resorted to creativity and effort,
one is released, just as a lion escapes from his cage.

16. In regard to the self,
the transitory nature of the body should be considered.
Beast-like behavior should be renounced
and one should resort in the delight of the self *(puruṣa).*

17. Do not reduce your energy to ashes
by indulging in the comforts
of a house full of women
and eating and drinking like a worm in a sore.

18. By pure creativity, pure results are gained quickly.
Impure always (follows) impure.
That which is called fate does not exist.

19. He who disregards what is evident
and relies on what is inferred (i.e., fate)
is like one who runs away from his own two hands
because they look like snakes.

20. "Fate propels me onwards!"
Such tormented thoughts
obscure the perception of the excellent.
Seeing thus, prosperity departs.

21. Therefore, through self-effort,
prior discrimination should be resorted to.
Knowledge of the self should be sought
in the meaning of the *śāstras.*

22. Thus the meaning of the *śāstras*
should be thought about in the mind,
with benefits in oneself.
The vain desires of the stupid accomplish nothing.

23. [It may be argued that:]
Creativity is without end,
effort is not to be desired.

Greatness is not obtained by effort
any more than a jewel from sand.

24. As with a perfect pot or a perfect weaving,
restraint, steady calculation, and human exertion
(are needed).

25. Through virtuous conduct, good company,
and (adherence to) the *śāstras*,
results are gained for oneself.
If one's nature is otherwise,
no goal is accomplished.

26. This is the conduct of self-formed creativity.
Anyone at any time (who lives in this way)
never goes lacking in fruitful effort.

27. Others among the highest of men,
who were formerly wretched, poverty stricken,
and distressed,
have become doers similar to the god Indra
by their creativity and effort.

28. By sufficiently studying the *śāstras*,
keeping good company, etc., from the time of childhood,
one's goal is attained
through these attributes and human effort.

29. This is apprehended through seeing,
perceiving, hearing, and experiencing.
The miserable and the stupid
think "It is from fate."

30. If there were not the worthlessness of sloth
in the world, who would not be wealthy or learned?
It is due to sloth that this ground between oceans
is full of poor and beast-like people.

31. After a man has spent his childhood continually in play,
let him, from the effort brought forth in his youth,
purify his mind as to the correct meaning of words and,

by good associations, let him examine his own faults
and qualities.

32. Srī Vālmīki said:
After the sage had spoken,
the day passed and we went home for the evening.
Then, having bathed and performed oblations,
we met again with the rising of the sun.

II:7 The Supreme Ability of Creativity (*Pauruṣa-prādhānya-samarthanaṃ*)

1. Vasiṣṭha said:
Once a body free from illness
and a mind whose pain is attenuated are obtained,
then, from fixing one's thought on the self,
one is not born again.
2. Whoever wishes to turn back fate by human action
has his wishes completely fulfilled
in this world and the other world.
3. Those who abandon their diligence
and take their last resort in fate
destroy all righteousness, wealth, and pleasure
and are their own enemy.
4. When the movement of consciousness, the movement
of mind, and the movement of the senses correspond
to the forms of human effort, then results arise.
5. When it desires sensation, consciousness, and movement,
then the body stirs and thus is enjoyer of results.
6. Even a child knows about success.
Fate is never seen;
hence, in this world there is creativity.
7. By human exertion Bṛhaspati became teacher of the gods.

By human exertion Sukra was elevated
to the position of the demon prince's teacher.

8. Though once afflicted, poverty stricken, and distressed,
the holy one who is best of men
by creativity and effort
became similar to the god Indra.

9. There are various reports of rich and powerful men
who, by exerting their creativity stupidly,
have become guests in hell
because of their behavior.

10. In the thousands, tens, and various (other instances)
of prosperity and misfortune, the bringing forth
of the world and its suppression *(nivṛttā)*
is from self-creativity and desire only.

11. There are three powers to draw from:
the *śāstras*, the teacher, and one's self.
Everywhere there is human exertion.
There is never fate.

12. In the case of being possessed by purity or impurity,
the mind, from persevering effort, would prevail.
Thus, the goal of all the *śāstras* is grasped.

13. That which is excellent,
not trifling, and which diminishes misfortunes
is, indeed, found through effort, son.

14. Wherever there is effort of mine,
results follow quickly.
From creativity I enjoy results,
not ever from fate.

15. From creativity, success is seen.
The power of the wise is from creativity.
In the fragile minds of the suffering,
comfort is found only in fate.

16. The power of creativity is always (seen)

through logic and by facing experience.
It is seen bearing fruit in the world
in someone going from one country to another.

17. The one who eats becomes full,
not the one who does not eat.
The one who goes somewhere travels,
not the one who does not move.
The speaker is heard,
not the one who keeps silent.
Thus (is seen) strong creativity and results.

18. Through creativity, those with good intellects
cross over danger and difficulty.
For others this is not so,
due to lack of effort and ineffectiveness.

19. Whoever exerts one's self
obtains the desired result.
But for the one who stands quietly,
indeed, what result is obtained?

20. The one who acts with pure purpose
meets with pure result.
Through the impure, impurity is obtained.
Thus, Rāma, do as you desire.

21. Due to human exertion, a result is obtained
from the desired place and time,
or with time it is gained quickly.
Others think this is fate.

22. There is no evidence for fate
seen here or in the other world.
By calling things fate, the fruits of action
are put into the world of heaven
(and are made inaccessible to the human order).

23. A man is born in this world,
grows up and ages.
There is no fate seen here,

merely the progression from childhood to old age.

24. According to the wise, highest effort
is the one means for obtaining a goal,
referred to by the word "creativity,"
by which everything is obtained.

25. Going from one place to another,
holding something in the hand:
these functions are by creativity of the limbs,
and are not due to fate.

26. But there are those for whom highest effort
obtains no goal.
It is said their efforts are misguided
and hence nothing is obtained.

27. Through action which has the nature of movement,
by the usefulness of one's own purpose,
by keeping good company, by following the *śāstras* keenly,
one is lifted upwards through thought.

28. Endless bliss and equanimity
are the highest goals of the wise one.
He obtains them through effort.
The virtues of the *śāstras* should be practiced.

29. By devotion, there (arises) the qualities
of following the *śāstras*, etc.
From the qualities of following the *śāstras*, etc.,
there is devotion.
From mutual practice it increases,
like a lotus grows with time.

30. It is by enough practices from the time of childhood
of keeping good company, studying the *śāstras*, etc.,
and by qualities with creativity and effort
that one's goal and welfare are accomplished.

31. It was by the creativity of Viṣṇu, not from fate,
that the demons were conquered, the actions of
the world were ordered, and beings were produced.

32. This world (arises) through action performed by a person.
Thus, Raghunātha (Rāma), perform great effort,
so as you go, you will not fear even the snakes
in the trees, O possessor of good fortune!

Notes

Chapter 1

1 Agehananda Bharati has been quite critical of the karma-reincarnation linkage, stating ". . . the way modern western scholars and most modern Indians use the word karma is a recent use, probably originating with the theosophists and Madame Blavatsky. Even the fabulous karma volumes edited by Wendy O'Flaherty and Karl Potter assume that this is the established meaning and their authors proceed from there, i.e., from the notion that karma is used predominantly in the sense of an impersonal law of positive and negative results due to previous actions and attitudes, thereby linking it to notions of rebirth. But this is not the traditional Indian use in any statistical sense, since in most places it means ritualistic action and only that. . . . [W]hen you talk to a grassroot Hindu who has not been exposed to English at all, he never uses the term karma in the modern sophisticated sense, even though modern, urban people in India, Sri Lanka, etc. do now so use it. But we simply do not know exactly which elements of karma talk are due to the theosophical import and which to indigenous import, once the latter is being marshalled in order to create momentum for a view that was originally imported from outside." (From "Speaking About 'That Which Shows Itself:' The Language of Mysticism and the Mystics,"

pp. 234-235, in *Religious Experience and Scientific Paradigms*, comp. Christopher Chapple, Stony Brook, New York: The Institute for Advanced Studies of World Religions, 1985, pp. 210-243.)

Similarly, Raimundo Panikkar has criticized modern interpretations of karma which identify it with reincarnation: "If there is something which the law of karman does not say and which contradicts all that it stands for, it is this popular misinterpretation. The law of karman insists that a man is: his energies, thoughts, merits, vices, his corporal elements and all that he was able to handle during his mortal life, that all the karmans do not get lost, rather they enter into the cosmic net of causality and solidarity. . . . What transmigrates is all but the individual if this word is to have any meaning at all. . . .

"I have witnessed more than once a simple Indian peasant, believing in the law of karman, being driven to say what he does not, in fact, believe. . . . he is not saying, and much less meaning, that it will be *he* that survives, that it is *his* personality that comes from somewhere else and goes to another. He has not the impression that what a modern would call the "individual" is what goes on transmigrating. . . . Life is what goes on. . . ." (From "The Law of Karman and the Historical Dimension of Man," p. 39, in *Philosophy East and West* 22, No. 1 (January, 1972):25-44).

2 For Buddhist sources on the power of recollecting past lives see Gregory Schopen, "The Generalization of an Old Yogic Attainment in Medieval Mahāyāna Sūtra Literature: Some Notes on *Jātismara*" (*Journal of the International Association of Buddhist Studies* 6, No. 1 (1983): 109-147). For reference to karma and rebirth in Jainism, see Padmanabh S. Jaini, *The Jaina Path of Purification* (Berkeley: University of California Press, 1979) and Helmuth von Glasenapp, *The Doctrine of Karma in Jain Philosophy* (Bombay: Bai Vijibai Jivanlal Panalal Charity Fund, 1942).

3 IV:4:3. Translations of this and other Upaniṣads are from the *The Thirteen Principal Upaniṣads Translated from the Sanskrit*, by Robert Ernest Hume (Oxford University Press, first published, 1921).

4 For more on karma in the *Dharmaśāstras*, see Ludo Rocher, "Karma and Rebirth in the Dharmaśāstras," in *Karma and Rebirth in Classical Indian Traditions*, ed. Wendy Doniger O'Flaherty (Berkeley: University of California Press, 1980) and Ariel Glucklich, "Theories of Karma in the Dharmaśāstra," doctoral dissertation, Harvard University, 1984.

5 *Avadāna Śataka* I:324.8.

6 J.N. Farquhar, *The Crown of Hinduism* (London: Oxford University Press, 1919), 143.

7 *Yoga Sūtra* (hereafter abbreviated as *YS*) II:12-14.

8 *YS* IV:7.

9 Madeleine Biardeau, "The Salvation of the King in the Mahābhārata" pp. 77, 96-97, in *Way of Life: King, Householder, Renouncer. Essays in Honour of Louis Dumont*, ed. T.N. Madan (New Delhi: Vikas, 1982), 75-98.

10 Mention of the importance of human effort over the seeming ravages of fate is found in Wendy Doniger O'Flaherty, ed., *Karma and Rebirth in Classical Indian Traditions*, 24, and in Koshelya Walli, *Theory of Karman in Indian Thought* (Varanasi: Bharata Manisha, 1977), 209.

Chapter 2

1 See W. Norman Brown, "The Creation Myth of the Ṛgveda," *Journal of the American Oriental Society* 62:85-98.

2 Wendy Doniger O'Flaherty, trans., *The Rig Veda: An Anthology* (Penguin Books, 1981), 25.

3 Antonio T. deNicolás, *Meditations Through the Ṛg Veda: Four Dimensional Man* (New York: Nicolas Hays, 1976), 74.

4 *Atharva Veda* XI.8.6.

5 Charles Malamoud, "Manyuḥ Svayambhūh," 506 in *Mélanges d'indianisme: A la memoire de Louis Renou* (Paris: Publications de l'Institut de Civilisation Indienne, 1968), 493-507.

6 J.C. Heesterman, summarizing the views of Oldenberg, Bergaigne, Silburn, Levi, and others, has described the Vedic ritual process as follows: "To the Vedic thinker the whole universe was constantly moving between two poles—of birth and death, integration and disintegration, ascension and descent—which by their interaction occasion the cyclical rhythms of the cosmos. In this world of floating forms there are no hard and fast lines: conceptually different entities and notions interchange with bewildering ease. . . . The point at issue for the Vedic thinker is not to disentangle and differentiate conceptually different entities and notions but to realize, to know, their connections *(bandhu-)*. . . . In the centre of this sacrificial world stands the sacrificer for whose benefit the cosmic processes are set in motion by the ritualists, who know the connections. Thus the whole world is centred upon the sacrificer, who 'becomes all this' and represents in his person the cosmic drama." From *The Ancient Royal Consecration: The Rājāsuya Described According to the Yajus Texts* (The Hague: Mouton,

1957), 6.

7 This story is found in Book VII, Section I. For a complete translation of this important text, see *The Śatapatha Brāhmaṇa According to the Text of the Mādhyandina School*, trans. Julius Eggeling (Delhi: Motilal Banarsidass, 1972; first published by the Clarendon Press, 1882) [Sacred Books of the East, Volumes 12, 26, 41, 43, 44].

8 *Śatapatha Brāhmaṇa* VI:2.2.27.

9 For more details on Indic biological analyses of creation processes, see "Karma, *Apūrva*, and 'Natural' Causes" by Wilhelm Halbfass in *Karma and Rebirth in Classical Indian Traditions*, ed. Wendy Doniger O'Flaherty (Berkeley: University of California Press, 1980), 268-302.

10 The most notable commentaries are the *Tattvakaumudī* of Vācaspatimiśra (ca. 850 C.E.) and the *Bhāṣya* of Gauḍapāda (ca. 1100 C.E.). Translations of Īśvarakṛṣṇa's text are given in S. Radhakrishnan's *A Source Book in Indian Philosophy* (Princeton University Press, 1957) and in Gerald Larson's *Classical Sāṃkhya* (2nd ed., Motilal Banarsidass, 1979).

11 Gerald James Larson, *Classical Sāṃkhya: An Interpretation of its History and Meaning* (Delhi: Motilal Banarsidass, 1969), 135.

Chapter 3

1 A general schematic of perceptual processes is summarized in the *Bhagavad Gītā* III:43. "They say the senses are important, but higher than the senses is the mind *(manas)*. Higher than the mind is intellect *(buddhi)* and even higher than the intellect is He." (The "He" refers to the unseen seer, the *puruṣa*.)

2 *Chāndogya Upaniṣad* III:18.1.

3 *Taittirīya Upaniṣad* III:3.

4 *Aitareya Upaniṣad* III:5.3.

5 *Kauṣītaki Upaniṣad* III:6; III:8.

6 *Maitri Upaniṣad* VI:34.

7 *Ibid.*

8 The most comprehensive presentations of Patañjali's text and its commentaries are Swāmi Hariharānanda Āraṇya's *Yoga Philosophy of Patañjali* (Albany: State University of New York Press, 1983) and James Haughton Woods' *The Yoga-System of Patañjali* (Cambridge, Mass.: Harvard

University Press, 1927).

9 *yogaś citta-vṛtti-nirodhaḥ.*

10 *avidyā-asmitā-rāga-dveṣa-abhiniveśa-kleśāh.*

11 *anitya-aśuci-duḥkha-anātmasu nitya-śuci-sukha-ātma-khyātir avidyā* [*Yoga Sūtra* II:5].

12 *Yoga Sūtra* II:12-14.

13 *Yoga Sūtra* II:15.

14 *Yoga Sūtra* II:11.

15 The openness of the yogic system is expressed in *Sūtra* I:39: "Or [yoga is achieved] by whatever meditation is suitable" [*yathā abhimata-dhyanād vā*].

16 Swāmi Hariharānanda Āraṇya, *Yoga Philosophy of Patañjali*, 101.

17 *Yoga Sūtra* I:41.

18 *Yoga Sūtra* I:43.

19 *Yoga Sūtra* I:47.

20 *Yoga Sūtra* I:50.

21 *Yoga Sūtra* IV:29.

22 *Yoga Sūtra* IV:15, 16.

23 Compare with *Sāṃkhya Kārikā* 64: "I am not, I own nothing, the 'I' does not exist."

24 *Bhagavad Gītā* XIII:29.

25 *Laṅkāvatāra Sūtra* II:204. These translations are my own. For a complete version of the text, see *The Lankavatara Sutra: A Mahayana Text*, trans. D.T. Suzuki (London: Routledge & Kegan Paul, 1956).

26 *Laṅkāvatāra Sūtra* III:75.

27 *Ibid.*, X:53.

28 *Ibid.*, X:277.

29 *Ibid.*, III:25.

30 *Ibid.*, III:121.

31 *Ibid.*, X:134.

32 *Ibid.*, X:239.

33 *Ibid.*, III:31.

34 The idea of inherent Buddha-nature or womb-of-suchness *(tathāgata-garbha)* resembles descriptions of self *(ātman)* in the Vedānta schools. See David Seyfort Ruegg, trans., *Le Traité du Tathāgatagarbha de Bu Ston Rin*

Chen Grub (Paris: École Française d'Extrême Orient, 1973).

35 For a summary translation of the text and an introductory essay on its history and development, see Swami Venkatesananda, *The Concise Yogavāsiṣṭha*, (Albany: SUNY Press, 1984). For an analysis of the dream stories in the *Yogavāsiṣṭha*, see Wendy Doniger O'Flaherty, *Dreams, Illusion, and Other Realities* (University of Chicago Press, 1984).

36 Several Sanskrit terms are used to indicate mind-only, including *citta-mātra, cittam eva, vijñānavāda, bhrānti-mātra,* and *mano-mātra.*

37 *Yogavāsiṣṭha* III:84.30. The translations are mine, using the edition of Wāsudeva Laxmana Śāstrī, *The Yogavāsiṣṭha of Vālmīki with the Commentary Vāsiṣṭhamahārāmāyaṇatātparyaprakāsha* (reprint, Munshiram Manoharlal, 1981).

38 *Ibid.*, VIB:59.48.

39 *Ibid.*, IV:20.3.

40 *Ibid.*, III:110.46-47.

41 *Ibid.*, IV:20.2.

42 *Ibid.*, III:91.4.

43 *Ibid.*, III:96.64.

44 *Ibid.*, III:96.71.

45 *Ibid.*, III:84.32.33.

46 *Ibid.*, IV:20.4.

47 *Ibid.*, III:84.35.

48 *Ibid.*, III:97.10.

49 *Ibid.*, III:95.2.

50 Ashok Kumar Chatterjee, *The Yogācāra Idealism* (Delhi: Motilal Banarsidass, 1975), 12.

51 Janice Dean Willis, *On Knowing Reality: The Tattvārtha Chapter of Asaṅga's Bodhisattvabhūmi* (New York: Columbia University Press, 1979), 25.

52 See also Thomas A. Kochumuttom, *A Buddhist Doctrine of Experience* (Delhi: Motilal Banarsidass, 1982).

53 Drawing from a vocabulary developed by O'Flaherty in her discussions of the *Yogavāsiṣṭha* and Magliola in his reading of Derrida, the texts of the mind-only tradition can be seen to posit a "soft" world, consisting of text, a world that is malleable through the techniques of yoga. Each individual is responsible for the etching on his or her own text; a text or world only becomes "hard" through desire and action. Seen through the prism of karma, life is a continuous record of inscriptions and erasures. For the com-

mon man or woman, the imprint of the past cannot be eradicated or even altered; the text remains as given and is taken subtly from circumstance to circumstance, all within the same inflexible world. For the man or woman of knowledge, on the other hand, nothing sticks to the ledger: karmas arise from nothing and pass into nothing. For the yogin or yoginī, karma is neither black nor white nor mixed. Having seen that the world is soft, that one is the author, and having abandoned attachment to fixed notions of self or other, the record of life becomes a movement and moment of creativity, informed by past actions but not bound by the letter.

Chapter 4

1 According to some early scholars of Indian literature, several innovative philosophical insights arose from the Kṣatriya caste, including Sāṃkhya. See A.B. Keith, *Religion and Philosophy of the Veda and the Upaniṣads* (Delhi: Motilal Banarsidass, 1976; first edition, 1925), 492-493 and M. Winternitz, *A History of Indian Literature* I, Part II: *Epics and Purāṇas*, 2nd ed. (University of Calcutta, 1963), 280.

2 For the complete story, see J.A.B. vanBuitenen, trans., *The Mahābhārata* III: *The Book of the Forest* (Chicago: The University of Chicago Press, 1975), 760-778. The text of the *Mahābhārata* reached its present form around 400 A.D., though some of the stories date from 1000 to 1500 years earlier.

3 J.A.B. vanBuitenen, trans., *The Mahābhārata* III: *The Book of the Forest* (Chicago: The University of Chicago Press, 1975), 772. The term "strict" is a translation of the Sanskrit word *sat*, which means existence or being. The usage here refers to someone who holds to things in their "isness" and is closely related to the term for truth *(satya)*. The feminine form *(satī)* refers to widows who follow their husbands onto the funeral pyre; Sāvitrī's story is an interesting variation in that she ventures after her husband into death and wins his return.

4 *Ibid.*, 778.

5 For a complete explanation of Vasiṣṭha's unusual birth, see *Ṛg Veda* VII:33 and Cornelia Dimmitt and J.A.B. vanBuitenen, *Classical Hindu Mythology: A Reader in the Sanskrit Purāṇas* (Philadelphia: Temple University Press, 1978), 265-267.

6 Other works with a Vasiṣṭhan title include the *Vasiṣṭhakalpa*, the *Vasiṣṭhatantra*, and the *Vasiṣṭhapurāṇa*. See T.G. Mainkar, *The Vasiṣṭha*

Rāmāyaṇa: A Study (New Delhi: Meharchand Lachhmandas, 1977), 157.

7 For references to other interpretations of *karma* in Indian literature, see "Karma and Rebirth in the Vedas and Purāṇas" by Wendy Doniger O'Flaherty and "The Concepts of Human Action and Rebirth in the *Mahābhārata*" by J. Bruce Long in *Karma and Rebirth in Classical Indian Traditions*, Wendy Doniger O'Flaherty, ed. (Berkeley: University of California Press, 1980).

8 *Mahābhārata* XIII:6.5-7. Translations are my own, based on the critical edition (Poona: Bhandarkar Oriental Research Institute, 1933-1972). For the complete chapter in translation, see Appendix I.

9 *Mahābhārata* XIII:6.8.

10 *Mahābhārata* XIII:6.9.

11 *Mahābhārata* XIII:6.10.

12 *Mahābhārata* XIII:6.34.

13 *Mahābhārata* XIII:6.30-40.

14 *Mahābhārata* XIII:6.13-14.

15 *Mahābhārata* XIII:6.27.

16 *Mahābhārata* XIII:6.11.

17 *Mahābhārata* XIII:6.15.

18 *Mahābhārata* XIII:6.17.

19 *Mahābhārata* XIII:6.20.

20 *Mahābhārata* XIII:6.19.

21 *Mahābhārata* XIII:6.42.

22 *Mahābhārata* XIII:6.41.

23 *Mahābhārata* XIII:6.40.

24 *Mahābhārata* XIII:6.43-44.

25 *Mahābhārata* XIII:6.47, 49.

26 See T.G. Mainkar, *The Vāsiṣṭha Rāmāyaṇa: A Study* (New Delhi: Meharchand Lachhmandas, 1977). Mainkar's research is supported in a recent article by Peter Thomi, "The Yogavāsiṣṭha in Its Longer and Shorter Versions" (*Journal of Indian Philosophy* 11, No. 1, 1983).

27 A complete English translation of the text is available, though the quality of the translation is poor: *The Yoga-Vāsiṣṭha-Mahā-Rāmāyaṇa of Vālmīki Translated from the Original Sanskrit*, Vihāri-Lāla Mitra (1st ed. 1891, 1893, 1898, 1899; reprint, Varanasi: Bharatiya Publishing House, 1976).

28 Fathullah Mojtaba'i, "Muntakhab'i Jug'basasht or Selecions from the Yoga Vāsiṣṭha Attributed to Mir Abu'l-gasim Findirski" (Doctoral Dissertation,

Harvard University, 1977), xiii, xxx.

29 *Yogavāsiṣṭha* I:12.7.

30 This follows the paradigm for religious life established by the Buddha. M. Winternitz, assuming that "the *Rāmāyaṇa* came into being at a time when Buddhism had already spread in Eastern India" goes so far to suggest Rāma "is more a sage after the heart of the Buddha, than a hero of war" [*A History of Indian Literature*, Volume I, Part II: *Epics and Purāṇas* (2nd ed., University of Calcutta, 1963), 448].

31 See the *Puruṣa Sukta* (*Ṛg Veda* X:90).

32 *Yogavāsiṣṭha* III:96.71.

33 For translations of this story, see Hari Prasad Shastri, *The World Within the Mind (Yoga-Vasistha): Extracts from the Discourses of the Sage Vasistha to his Pupil, Prince Rama, and the Story of Queen Chudala* (London: The Favil Press, 1937) and Peter Thomi, *Cūdālā: Eine Episode aus dem Yogavāsiṣṭha* (Wichtrach, Switzerland: Institut für Indologie, 1980).

34 *Yogavāsiṣṭha* II:7.28. Most of the material cited here is from Chapters 4, 5, and 7 of the *Mumukṣuprakaraṇa*, which are translated in Appendix II.

35 *Yogavāsiṣṭha* II:4.11. Hereafter, *Yogavāsiṣṭha* will be abbreviated as *YV*.

36 *YV* II:5.16-17.

37 *YV* II:4.19.

38 *YV* II:5.14.

39 *YV* II:7.29.

40 *YV* II:9.36-38.

41 "The mental natures are the result of what we have thought, are chieftained by our thoughts, are made up of our thoughts. If a man speaks or acts with an evil thought, sorrow follows him (as a consequence) even as the wheel follows the foot of the drawer (i.e., the ox which draws the cart)." *Dhammapada* I, S. Radhakrishnan, trans.

42 *YV* II:5.18; II:7.20.

43 *YV* II:5.11.

44 *YV* II:7.12.

45 *YV* II:4.17.

46 *YV* II:5.5.

47 *YV* II:5.19.

48 *YV* II:5.12.

49 *YV* II:4.10.

50 *YV* II:5.3.

51 *YV* II:5.13.

52 *YV* II:5.20.

53 *YV* II:5.23.

54 *YV* II:5.24.

55 *YV* II:5.30.

56 *YV* II:7.3.

57 *YV* II:7.16-17.

58 *YV* II:7.23.

59 *YV* II:7.22.

60 *YV* II:7.14-15.

61 *YV* II:7.19.

62 *YV* II:7.9.

63 B.L. Atreya, *Deification of Man: Its Methods and Stages According to Yogavāsiṣṭha*, 2nd ed. (Moradabad, India: Darshana Printers, 1963), 8.

64 *YV* II:4.13-16.

65 See Agehananda Bharati, *The Tantric Tradition* (New York: Doubleday, 1967).

66 *YV* II:4.4-5.

67 *YV* II:4.3.

68 B.L. Atreya, *The Yogavāsiṣṭha and Its Philosophy*, 3rd ed. (Moradabad: Darshana Printers, 1966), 56-59.

69 *YV* II:5.15.

70 *YV: VIB:199.31, VIB:174.24, VIB:197.18.*

71 *YV* III:5, 6-7.

Chapter 5

1 *Yogavāsiṣṭha* VIB:213.50.

2 Marriott and Inden refer to this Vedic figure as Code Man. Because he carries all the castes within his body (brahmans are his mouth, kṣatriyas his arms, vaiśyas his thighs, śūdras his feet [see *Ṛg Veda* X:90]), he is seen as symbolizing the underlying unity of Hindu social transactions. See McKim Marriott and Ronald B. Inden, "Caste Systems," *Encyclopedia Britannica*, 15th ed. (Chicago, 1975), Macropaedia III, 983.

3 For a comprehensive philosophical study of the *Bhagavad Gītā*, including translation, see Antonio T. deNicolás, *Avatāra: The Humanization of Philosophy through the Bhagavad Gītā* (New York: Nicolas Hayes, 1976). For an analysis of the Sanskrit text, see *The Bhagavad Gītā: An Interlinear Translation*, Winthrop Sargeant, trans. Christopher Chapple ed. (Albany: SUNY Press, 1984).

4 J.A.B. vanBuitenen, *The Mahābhārata 1. The Book of the Beginning* (Chicago: University of Chicago Press, 1974), xxv.

5 Madeleine Biardeau, *Études de Mythologie hindoue. Tome I. Cosmogonies Purāṇiques* (Paris: École Française d'Extrême Orient, 1981), 147-148. For more on the idea of continuity of life in the Hindu tradition, see Charles Malamoud, "Observations sur la notion de 'reste' dans le brāhmanisme" in *Wiener Zeitschrift für kunde des Süd-Asiens und Archiv für indische Philosophie* (Wien, Vol. 16 [1972], 5-26).

Appendix 1

* Based on *The Mahābhārata, For the First Time Critically Edited*, by Vishnu S. Sukthankar and others, Fascicule 34 (Poona: Bhandarkar Oriental Research Institute, 1963).

Appendix 2

* Based on *The Yogavāsiṣṭha of Vālmīki with the Commentary Vāsiṣṭha-mahārāmāyaṇatātparyaprakāsha*, ed. Wāsudeva Laxmaṇa Pansīkar, Second Edition (Bombay: Nirnaya-Sagar Press, 1918; reprinted, New Delhi: Munshiram Manoharlal, 1981).

Bibliography

SELECTED TEXT EDITIONS AND TRANSLATIONS:

Anthologies

Pereira, Jose. *Hindu Theology: A Reader*. Garden City, New York: Image Books, 1976.

Radhakrishnan, Sarvepalli and Charles A. Moore, editors. *A Source Book in Indian Philosophy*. Princeton, New Jersey: Princeton University Press, 1957.

Atharva Veda

Whitney, William Dwight, trans. *Atharva-Veda Samhitā: Translated with a Critical and Exegetical Commentary*. Revised and brought nearer to completion and edited by Charles Rockwell Lanman. Cambridge, Massachusetts: Harvard University, 1905. (*Harvard Oriental Series*, Vols. VII and VIII.)

Bhagavad Gītā

Sargeant, Winthrop, trans. *The Bhagavad Gītā*. Revised edition.

Edited by Christopher Chapple. Foreword by Swami Samatananda. Albany: State University of New York Press, 1984.

vanBuitenen, J.A.B., trans. *The Bhagavad Gītā in the Mahābhārata: Text and Translation.* Chicago: The University of Chicago Press, 1981.

Laṅkāvatāra Sūtra

Nanjio, Bunyiu, ed. *The Laṅkāvatāra Sūtra.* [In Sanskrit.] Kyoto: Otani University Press, 1923.

Suzuki, Daisetz Teitara, trans. *The Laṅkāvatāra Sūtra, A Mahāyāna Text.* London: George Routledge and Sons, 1932.

Mahābhārata

Dandekar, Ramachandra Narayan, ed. *The Anuśāsanaparvan, Being the Thirteenth Book of the Mahābhārata, The Great Epic of India.* Poona: Bhandarkar Oriental Research Institute, 1966.

Sukthankar, Vishnu S., ed. *The Āraṇyakaparvan (Part 2), Being the Third Book of the Mahābhārata, The Great Epic of India.* Poona: Bhandarkar Oriental Research Institute, 1942.

vanBuitenen, J.A.B., trans. *The Mahābhārata. 1. The Book of the Beginning.* Chicago: The University of Chicago Press, 1973.

__________. *The Mahābhārata. 2. The Book of the Assembly Hall. 3. The Book of the Forest.* Chicago: The University of Chicago Press, 1975.

__________. *The Mahābhārata. 4. The Book of Virāṭa. 5. The Book of Effort.* Chicago: The University of Chicago Press, 1978.

Vyasa, Krishna-Dwaipayana. *The Mahabharata of Krishna-Dwaipayana Vyasa Translated into English Prose.* [Translator not given.] Calcutta: Bharata Press, 1893.

Ṛg Veda

Griffith, Ralph T.H. *The Hymns of the Ṛgveda, Translated with a Popular Commentary.* Delhi: Motilal Banarsidass, 1973 (reprint).

O'Flaherty, Wendy Doniger. *The Rig Veda: An Anthology.* London: Penguin Books, 1981.

Sāṃkhya Kārikā

Jhā, Gaṅgānātha, trans. *The Tattva-kaumudī: Vācaspati Miśra's Commentary on the Sāṃkhya Kārikā.* Bombay: Theosophical Publishing Fund, 1896. Third Edition, Poona: Oriental Book Agency, 1965.

Sharma, Har Dutt, trans. *The Sāṃkhya Kārikā: Iśvara Kṛṣṇa's Memorable Verses on Sāṃkhya Philosophy with the Commentary of Gauḍapadācarya.* Poona: Oriental Book Agency, no date given.

Śatapatha Brāhmaṇa

Eggeling, Julius, trans. *The Śatapatha Brāhmaṇa According to the Text of the Mādhyandina School.* Delhi: Motilal Banarsidass, 1972. First published by the Clarendon Press, 1882. *(Sacred Books of the East,* Volumes 12, 26, 41, 43, 44.)

Upaniṣads

The Bṛhadāraṇyaka Upaniṣad, Containing the Original Text with Word-by-word Meaning, Running Translation, Notes and Introduction. Madras: Sri Ramakrishna Math, 1968. *(Upaniṣad Series.)*

Hume, Robert Ernest. *The Thirteen Principal Upaniṣads.* Second edition, revised. London: Oxford University Press, 1931.

Yoga Sūtra

Āraṇya, Swāmi Hariharānanda, trans. *Yoga Philosophy of Patañjali: Containing His Yoga Aphorisms with Vyāsa's Commentary in Sanskrit and a Translation with Annotations Including Many Suggestions for the Practice of Yoga.* Translated into English by P.N. Mukerji. Albany: State University of New York Press, 1983. First published by Calcutta University Press, 1963.

Chapple, Christopher, Yogi Anand Viraj, William Bilodeau, Sal Familia, trans. *The Yoga Sūtra of Patañjali. Book One: Samādhi Pāda, An Analysis of the Sanskrit with Accompanying English Translation.* Amityville, New York: Vajra Press, 1984.

Feuerstein, Georg, trans. *The Yoga Sūtra of Patañjali: A New Translation and Commentary.* Kent, U.K.: Dawson, 1979.

Rukmani, T.S., trans. *Yogavārttika of Vijñānabhikṣu: Text along with English Translation and Critical Notes along with the Text and English Translation of the Pātañjala Yogasūtras and Vyāsabhyāṣa. Vol. 1: Samādhipāda.* New Delhi: Munshiram Manoharlal, 1981. *Vol. 2: Sādhanapāda.* New Delhi: Munshiram Manoharlal, 1983.

Woods, James Haughton, trans. *The Yoga-System of Patañjali or the Ancient Hindu Doctrine of Concentration of Mind Embracing the Mnemonic Rules, Called Yoga-Sūtras, of Patañjali and the Comment, Called Yoga-Bhāshya, Attributed to Veda-Vyāsa and the Explanation, Called Tattva-Vāiçāradi, of Vāchaspati-Miçra.* Cambridge, Massachusetts: Harvard University Press, 1927.

Yogavāsiṣṭha

Mitra, Vihāri-Lāla, trans. The Yoga-Vāsishtha-Mahārāmāyana of Vālmiki Translated for the Original Sanskrit. In four volumes. Varanasi: Bharatiya Publishing House, 1976. First edition, published in Calcutta, 1891, 1893, 1898, 1899.

Panśīkar, Wāsudeva Laxamana Śāstrī, ed. *The Yogavāsiṣṭha of Vālmiki with the Commentary Vāsiṣṭhamahārāmayaṇatātparya-prakāsha.* Bombay: Nirnaya-Sāgar Press, 1911. Second edition, 1918. Third edition, revised and re-edited by Nārāyan Rām Āchārya Kāvyatīrtha, 1937. Reprinted by Munshiram Manoharlal, New Delhi, 1981.

Venkatesananda, Swami, trans. *The Concise Yoga Vāsiṣṭha.* With an Introduction and Bibliography by Christopher Chapple. Albany: State University of New York Press, 1984.

Secondary Sources:

Atreya, B.L. *Deification of Man: Its Methods and Stages According to the Yogavāsiṣṭha.* Second Edition. Moradabad: Darshana, 1963.

__________. *The Philosophy of the Yogavāsiṣṭha.* Adyar: The Theosophical Publishing House, 1936.

__________. *The Yogavāsiṣṭha and Its Philosophy.* Moradabad: Darshana, 1966.

Biardeau, Madeleine. "Ahaṃkāra: The Ego Principle in the Upaniṣad." *Contributions to Indian Sociology* VIII (1965): 62-84.

__________. *Études de Mythologie Hindoue.* Tome I, *Cosmogonies Purāṇiques.* Paris: École Française d'Extrême Orient, 1981. *(Publications de l'École Française d'Extrême Orient* CXXVIII.)

__________. "The Salvation of the King in the Mahābhārata." In T.N. Madan, editor, *Way of Life: King, Householder, Renouncer. Essays in Honour of Louis Dumont.* New Delhi: Vikas Publishing House, 1982. *(Contributions to Indian Sociology* XV.)

Biardeau, Madeleine and Charles Malamoud. *Le Sacrifice dans l'Inde Ancienne.* Paris: Presses Universitaires de France, 1976. *(Bibliothèque de l'École des Hautes Études, Section des Sciences Religeuses* LXXIX.)

Bharati, Agehananda. *The Tantric Tradition.* New York: Doubleday, 1967.

Bhattacharji, Sukumari. *The Indian Theogony: A Comparative Study of Indian Mythology from the Vedas to the Purāṇas.* Cambridge: University Press, 1970.

Brown, W. Norman. "The Creation Myth of the Ṛg Veda." *Journal of the American Oriental Society* 62 (1942): 85-98.

Chakravarti, Pulinibihari. *Origin and Development of the Sāṃkhya System of Thought.* New Delhi: Oriental Reprint, 1975.

Chapple, Christopher, "Citta-vṛtti and Reality in the Yoga Sūtra."In Christopher Chapple, editor, *Sāṃkhya-Yoga: Proceedings of the IASWR Conference, 1981.* Stony Brook, New York: The Institute for Advanced Studies of World Religions, 1983, pp. 103-119.

__________. "The Concept of Will (Pauruṣa) in the Yogavāsiṣṭha." Doctoral dissertation, Fordham University, 1980.

__________. "The Negative Theology of the Yogavāsiṣṭha and the Laṅkāvatāra Sūtra." *Journal of Dharma* VI (1981): 34-45.

__________. "The Pauruṣa Paradigm of the Yogavāsiṣṭha." *Journal of Religious Studies* IX (1981): 47-61.

__________, comp. *Religious Experience and Scientific Paradigms: Proceedings of the IASWR Conference, 1982.* Stony Brook, New York: The Institute for Advanced Studies of World Religions, 1985.

Chatterjee, Ashok Kumar. *The Yogacara Idealism.* Delhi: Motilal Banarsidass, 1975.

Chethimattam, John B. *Patterns of Indian Thought*. London: G. Chapman, 1971.

Chethimattam, John B. and Antonio T. deNicolás. *A Philosophy in Song-poems: Selected Poems from the Rigveda*. Bangalore: Dharmaram, 1971.

Conze, Edward. *Buddhist Thought in India: Three Phases of Buddhist Philosophy*. Ann Arbor, Michigan: The University of Michigan Press, 1967.

Coomeraswamy, Ananda K. *Spiritual Authority and Temporal Power in the Indian Theory of Government*. New Haven, Connecticut: American Oriental Society, 1942.

Coward, Harold. "Mysticism in the Analytical Psychology of Carl Jung and the Yoga Psychology of Patanjali: A Comparative Study." *Philosophy East and West* XXIX (1979): 323-336.

__________. "Psychology and Karma." *Philosophy East and West* XXXIII(1983): 49-60.

Dasgupta, Surendranath. *A History of Indian Philosophy*. Five volumes. Cambridge University Press, 1932.

_________. *Indian Idealism*. Cambridge: Cambridge University Press, 1933.

deNicolás, Antonio T. *Avatāra: The Humanization of Philosophy Though the Bhagavad Gītā*. New York: Nicolas Hays, 1976.

__________. *Four Dimensional Man: The Philosophical Methodology of the Rig Veda*. Bangalore: Dharmaram College, 1971.

__________. *Meditations Through the Ṛg Veda*. New York: Nicolas Hays, 1976.

deSmet, Richard. "Copernican Reversal: Gītakāra's Reformulation of Karma." *Philosophy East and West* XXVII (1977): 53-63.

Deutsch, Eliot. "Karma as a 'Convenient Fiction' in the Advaita Vedanta." *Philosophy East and West* XV (1965): 3-12.

Dimmit, Cornelia and J.A.B. vanBuitenen. *Classical Hindu Mythology: A Reader in the Sanskrit Purāṇas*. Philadelphia: Temple University Press, 1978.

Dimock, Edward C., editor. *The Literatures of India: An Introduction*. Chicago: The University of Chicago Press, 1974.

Dumont, Louis. *Homo Hierarchicus: The Caste System and Its Implications*. Translated by Mark Sainsbury. Chicago: The University of Chicago Press, 1970.

Eliade, Mircea. *Patanjali and Yoga*. New York: Schocken Books, 1975.

__________. *Yoga: Immortality and Freedom.* Princeton, New Jersey: Princeton University Press, 1969.

Farquhar, John Nichol. *The Crown of Hinduism.* London: Oxford University Press, 1919.

__________. *An Outline of the Religious Literature of India.* London: Oxford University Press, 1920.

Glucklich, Ariel. "Theories of Karma in the Dharmaśāstra." Doctoral dissertation, Harvard University, 1984.

Goldman, Robert P. *The Rāmāyaṇa of Vālmīki: An Epic of Ancient India.* Volume I. *Bālakāṇḍa.* Princeton, New Jersey: Princeton University Press, 1984.

Gonda, Jan. *Ancient Indian Kingship from the Religious Point of View.* Leiden: E.J. Brill, 1966.

__________. *Change and Continuity in Indian Religion.* The Hague: Mouton, 1965.

Guenther, Herbert. "Samvṛti and Paramartha in Yogacara According to Tibetan Sources." In Mervyn Sprung, editor, *The Problem of Two Truths in Buddhism and Vedanta.* Dordvecht, Holland: D. Reidel, 1973.

Heesterman, J.C. *The Ancient Indian Royal Consecration: The Rājāsuya Described According to the Yajus Texts and Annotated.* The Hague: Mouton, 1957.

Hopkins, Thomas J. *The Hindu Religious Tradition.* Belmont, California: Dickenson, 1971.

Jaini, Padmanabh S. *The Jaina Path of Purification.* Berkeley: University of California Press, 1979.

Karmarkar, R.D. "Mutual Relation of the Yogavāsiṣṭha, the Laṅkāvatārasūtra and the Gauḍapada-kārikās." *Annals of the Bhandarkar Oriental Research Institute, Poona* 36 (1955): 298-305.

Keith, Arthur Berriedale. *The Religion and Philosophy of the Veda and the Upaniṣads.* First edition, 1925. Delhi: Motilal Banarsidass, 1975.

__________. *The Sāṃkhya System: A History of the Sāṃkhya Philosophy.* Mysore City: Wesleyan Mission Press, 1918.

Keyes, Charles F. and E. Valentine Daniel, editors. *Karma: An Anthropological Inquiry.* Berkeley: University of California Press, 1983.

Klaes, Norbert. *Conscience and Consciousness.* Bangalore:

Dharmaram, 1975.

Kochumuttom, Thomas A. *A Buddhist Doctrine of Experience: A New Translation and Interpretation of the Works of Vasubandhu the Yogācārin.* Delhi: Motilal Banarsidass, 1982.

Larson, Gerald J. *Classical Sāṃkhya: An Interpretation of Its History and Meaning.* Delhi: Motilal Banarsidass, 1969.

Lévi, Sylvain. *Matériaux pour l'Étude du Système Vijñaptimātra.* Paris: Librarie Ancienne, 1932.

Magliola, Robert. *Derrida on the Mend.* West Lafayette, Indiana: Purdue University Press, 1984.

Malamoud, Charles. "Manyuḥ Svayambhūḥ." In *Mélanges d'Indianisme: A la Mémoire de Louis Renou.* Paris: Publications de l' Institut de Civilisation Indienne, 1968, 493-507.

__________. "Observations sur la Notion de 'Reste' dans le Brāhmanisme." *Wiener Zeitschrift für kunde des Süd-Asiens und Archiv für indische Philosophie* XVI (1972): 5-26.

Mainkar, T.G. *The Vāsiṣṭha Rāmāyaṇa: A Study.* New Delhi: Meharchand Lachhmandas, 1977.

Marriott, McKim. "Hindu Transactions: Diversity without Dualism." In Bruce Kapferer, editor, *Transaction and Meaning: Directions in the Anthropology of Exchange and Symbolic Behavior.* Philadelphia: Institute for the Study of Human Issues, 1976, 109-142.

Marriott, McKim and Ronald B. Inden. "Caste Systems." *Encyclopaedia Britannica.* 15th edition. Macropaedia III, 982-991.

McClain, Ernest G. *The Myth of Invariance.* New York: Nicolas Hays, 1972.

McMichael, James Douglas. "Idealism in Yoga-Vāsiṣṭha and Yogācāra Buddhism." *Darshana International* XVII (1977).

Mojtaba'i, Fathullah. "Muntakhab'i Jug-basasht or Selections from the Yogāvāsiṣṭha Attributed to Mir Abu'l-qasim Findirski." Doctoral dissertation, Harvard University, 1977.

Narahari, H.G. "The Yogavasistha and the Doctrine of Free Will." *Adyar Library Bulletin* X(1946): 36-50.

Nikhilananda, Swami, trans. *The Māṇḍūkyopaniṣad with Gauḍapada's Kārikā and Śankara's Commentary.* Mysore: Ramakrishna Ashrama, 1936.

O'Flaherty, Wendy Doniger. *Dreams, Illusion and Other Realities.* Chicago: The University of Chicago Press, 1984.

__________, editor. *Karma and Rebirth in Classical Indian Traditions.* Berkeley: University of California Press, 1980.

Panikkar, Raymond. "The Law of Karman and the Historical Dimension of Man." *Philosophy East and West* XXII (1972): 25-44.

Podgorski, Frank R. *Ego, Revealer-Concealer: A Key to Yoga.* Lanham, Maryland: University Press of America, 1984.

Robinson, Richard H. *The Buddhist Religion.* Belmont, California: Dickenson, 1970.

Ruegg, David Seyfort. *Le Traité du Tathāgatagarbha de Bu Ston Rin Chen Grub.* Paris: École Française d'Extrême Orient, 1973. (*Publications de l'École Française d'Extrême Orient* LXXXVIII.)

Schopen, Gregory. "The Generalization of an Old Yogic Attainment in Medieval Mahayana Sutra Literature: Some Notes on *Jātismara.*" *Journal of the International Association of Buddhist Studies* 6 (1983): 109-147.

Sengupta, Anima. *Classical Sāṃkhya: A Critical Study.* Patna: Patna University, 1969.

Shastri, Hari Prasad. *Yogavasistha: The Story of Queen Chudala and Sermons of Holy Vasistha.* London: The Favil Press, 1937.

Sinha, Jadunath. *A History of Indian Philosophy.* Calcutta: Calcutta Publishing House, 1956.

Srivastava, R.S., editor. *The Philosophy of Dr. B.L. Atreya.* New Delhi: Oriental Publishers, 1977.

Stcherbatsky, Theodore. *The Central Conception of Buddhism and the Meaning of the World "Dharma."* London: Royal Asiatic Society, 1923.

Thomi, Peter. *Cūḍālā: Eine Episode aus dem Yogavāsiṣṭha.* Wichtrach, Switzerland: Institut für Indologie, 1980.

Tripathi, Chhote Lal. *The Problem of Knowledge in Yogācāra Buddhism.* Varanasi: Bhavat Bharati, 1972.

Varenne, Jean. *Yoga and the Hindu Tradition.* Translated by Derek Coltman. Chicago: University of Chicago Press, 1976.

von Glasenapp, Helmuth. *The Doctrine of Karma in Jain Philosophy.* Bombay: Bai Vijibai Jivanlal Charity Fund, 1942.

__________. *Zwei philosophische Rāmāyanas.* Wiesbaden: Steiner, 1951. (*Akademie der Wissenschaften und der Literatur in Mainz. Abhandlungen der geistes — und sozialwissenschaftlichen Klasse* VI.)

Walli, Koshelya. *Theory of Karman in Indian Thought.* Varanasi: Bharata Manisha, 1977.

Wayman, Alex. "The Yogacara Idealism." *Philosophy East and West* XV (1965): 65-73.

Willis, Janice Dean. *On Knowing Reality: The Tattvārtha Chapter of Asaṅga's Bodhisattvabhūmi.* New York: Columbia University Press, 1979.

Glossary and Index of Sanskrit Terms

adharma, non-virtue; one of the eight *bhāvas* of *buddhi*, 27

adhyātma, inner self, 42

āgama, valid testimony; one of the three means of knowledge, 37

agni, Vedic god of fire, 13

ahaṃkāra, sense-of-I; literally, I-maker; sometimes translated as ego, 24-26, 33, 37-38, 43-44

ahiṃsā, non-violence, 2, 40

aihika, present time, 71

aiśvarya, power, strength; one of the eight *bhāvas*, 27

ajñana, ignorance, 27

akṣara, the imperishable; epithet for Brahman, 18, 87

ālaya-vijñāna, store-house consciousness; receptacle of past impressions in Yogācāra Buddhism, 49

anaiśvarya, weakness; opposite of *aiśvarya;* one of the eight *bhāvas*, 27

anumāna, inference, 37

aparigraha, nonpossession, 40

artha, purpose, goal; also means wealth, 5

asaṃprajñatā, state of yoga without object of meditation, 42

āsana, yoga posture, 41

asat, non-existence, 10-11, 13

asmitā, egoism; literally, I-am-ness, 2, 38, 43

āśrama, retreat for meditation; hermitage, 76, 92

desire; enlightenment, 1, 2, 8, 45-46, 66, 82, 91
nirvastuka, free of object; used to describe meditation states in Yoga, 44
nirvicāra, free from reflection, 42
nirvitarka, free from thought, 41
nivṛtti, cessation; abstaining from worldly acts, 111
niyama, observances; one of the eight limbs of yoga, 40
pauruṣa, creativity, 53, 64, 67-68, 72, 103, 110
phala, fruit; result, 4, 86
prajñā, intelligence; wisdom, 35
prāktana, the past, 71
prakṛti, the creative aspect of reality in Sāṃkhya, composed of the three *guṇas*, 22-34, 37, 39, 42-51, 67, 79, 83, 87, 89, 90, 92
pramāṇa, valid cognition, 37
prāṇa, breath; life force, 21
prāṇāyāma, control of breath; one of the eight limbs of Yoga, 41
pratipakṣa-bhāvanaṃ, cultivation of opposite; recommended in *Yoga Sūtra* to overcome inhibiting thoughts
pratyāhāra, detachment, 41
pratyakṣa, direct perception, 37
pravṛtti, active life; involvement with world, 106
prayatna, effort, 67
puruṣa, the silent, witnessing, non-creative consciousness; also means man or human, 7, 13, 16-17, 19, 21-38, 44, 49-51, 67, 79, 83, 87, 89-91, 94, 108
puruṣa-kāra, human effort, 59, 60, 72
puruṣārtha, goal of human pursuit; human exertion, 71, 104
puruṣottama, the highest *puruṣa* (see above), 88
rāga, attachment, 2, 27
rājārṣi, philosopher-king; sage ruler, 82
rajas, activity, excitement, passion; one of the three *guṇas*, 23, 24, 86
ṛṣi, seer or sage, 13, 16, 84
ṛta, norm; social order; truth, 10-12
sadācāra, good conduct, 69
sādhu, good man; holy person, 63, 68, 104
śama, peace, tranquility, 87
samādhi, state of absorption; eighth limb of Yoga, 41-44, 47, 51
saṃkalpa, conception; intention, 19
saṃprajñatā, state of Yoga using object for meditation, 41
saṃsāra, round of existence; worldly life, 1, 2, 36, 45, 75, 78, 91, 104
saṃskāra, impression left from past action, residue, 5, 37, 42, 47, 49
saṃtoṣa, contentment, 40
sannyāsin, renunciate, 75, 86, 89, 92
sarga, emergence of the world; manifestation, 38
sarva, everything; all, 66
śāstra, sacred writing or teaching, 68-69, 71, 74, 78, 82, 95, 105-109, 113
sat, existence, 10, 11
satsaṅga, good company, 69
sattva, lightness; one of the three *guṇas*, 23-24
sattvika, having the quality of *sattva*, 27
satya, truth, 19, 40
śauca, purity, 40

General Index